Paddlewheels on the Upper Mississippi: 1823–1854

How Steamboats Promoted Commerce and Settlement in the West

by Nancy and Robert Goodman

With 255 individual boat histories and more than 70 illustrations.

Published for the History Network of Washington County
by the Washington County Historical Society

Printed by University of Minnesota Printing Services
October 2003

Published October 2003
for the History Network of Washington County
by the Washington County Historical Society,
Stillwater, Minnesota

Order from:

      Washington County Historical Society
      P.O. Box 167
      Stillwater, Minnesota 55082-0167
      651-439-5956
      e-mail: information@wchsmn.org

This publication was funded in part by grants from the Minnesota-Wisconsin Boundary Area Commission and James Taylor Dunn, with additional contributions from Burton Wahlquist and the Washington County Historical Society.

Printed in the United States of America by the University of Minnesota Printing Services.

First edition

ISBN Number 0-9708328-1- 8
Library of Congress Card Catalog Number 2003113955

Front cover: *War Eagle* with an excursion party, from the collections of the Winona County Historical Society; back cover: steamboat tickets from the collection of the Battle of Lexington State Historic Site, Lexington, Missouri.

Dedicated
to James Taylor Dunn (1912-2002)

For his enthusiasm for Minnesota and valley history;
his willingness to share his knowledge;
his eagerness to assist other researchers;
his skill at bringing history alive; and
his financial support that has made this, and so
many other history books and projects, possible.

James Taylor Dunn
Photo by Donald Empson

With additional thanks to . . .

Brent Peterson, Washington County Historical Society Executive Director, who served as project director; Lee Bjerk, Images of the Past of Stillwater, who supplied photographic expertise; William E. Lass, emeritus professor of history at the Minnesota State University, Mankato, whose counsel as advisor to the project was invaluable; Anita Buck and Judy Yaeger Jones, Minnesota scholars, who read the manuscript and offered illuminating suggestions; and Clarence W. Malick, whose vision inspired the project.

Thanks also to all the people who helped researchers locate photographs and reference materials, especially: Tacie Campbell, Mississippi Riverboat Museum, Dubuque; Eunice Schlicting, Putnam Museum and Archives, Davenport; Betty Gorden, St. Louis Mercantile Library, University of Missouri St. Louis; Darrell Watson, Galena Historical Museum, Galena; Walter Bennick, Winona County (MN) Historical Society; M'Lissa Kesterman, Public Library of Cincinnati and Hamilton County, Cincinnati; Ellen Thomasson, Missouri Historical Society, St. Louis; and the helpful staffs at the Murphy Library Area Research Center, University of Wisconsin–La Crosse; State Historical Society of Missouri, Columbia; the Minnesota Historical Society, St. Paul; and the State Historical Society of Wisconsin, Madison.

How This Book Came to Be

This project was originally conceived in late 2000 by Clarence E. (Buck) Malick, executive director of the Minnesota-Wisconsin Boundary Area Commission (MWBAC). Fourteen regional and local historical organizations had already endorsed the project, authors had committed their time and much of the preliminary research had been done when the MWBAC lost its funding during the 2002 budget session. Malick suggested that the History Network of Washington County take over publication of the book, with the Washington County Historical Society to serve as fiscal agent and publisher. Both organizations approved the project. A steering committee of History Network members was formed, met and gave the project a new and broader scope, as the MWBAC focus had been on only the Minnesota-Wisconsin border rivers. It became a truly collaborative project.

Volunteers canvassed historical organizations with river orientation to locate manuscript sources and photos. The steering committee contacted many historical organizations up and down the river for local history contributions. Through an MWBAC grant, researchers visited major steamboat collections in Cincinnati, Madison, La Crosse, Galena, Davenport, St. Louis, Burlington, Dubuque and Winona, as well as many local organizations in the river corridor. A comprehensive list of sources that have been consulted is in the bibliography.

Supporting Historical Organizations

Arcola Mills Center, Marine
Buffalo County (WI) Historical Society
Chisago County (MN) Historical Society
Goodhue County (MN) Historical Society
Grant County (WI) Historical Society
History Network of Washington County (MN)
Houston County (MN) Historical Society
Lake City (MN) Historical Society
Lower Wisconsin Genealogical and Historical Research Center, Wauzeka
Pepin County (WI) Historical Society
Prescott Area (WI) Historical Society
St. Croix Falls (WI) Historical Society
St. Croix County (WI) Historical Society
Vernon County (WI) Historical Society
Washington County (MN) Historical Society
Winona County (MN) Historical Society

History Network of Washington County

This project is a collaborative effort of the members of the History Network of Washington County, an informal association of historical societies, historic sites and other organizations within the county and in nearby communities.

Afton Historical Museum
Arcola Mills Center, Marine
ArtReach Alliance
Bayport Public Library
Cottage Grove Advisory Committee on Historic Preservation
Denmark Township Heritage Society
Gammelgården Museum, Scandia
Grant Township Historical Society
Hugo Heritage Society
Marine Restoration Society
Minnesota Historical Society
Newport Heritage Preservation Commission
Oakdale-Lake Elmo Historical Society
Pierce County, Wisconsin, Historical Society
Polk County, Wisconsin, Historical Society
Prescott (Wisconsin) Area Historical Society
RiverTown Restoration, Inc., Stillwater
South Washington Heritage Society
St. Croix County (Wisconsin) Historical Society
St. Croix Valley Civil War Round Table
St. Croix River Association
St. Croix Valley Alliance for Tourism
Stillwater Public Library
Stillwater Heritage Preservation Commission
Stone House Museum, Marine on St. Croix
Valley Tours, Stillwater
Washington County Historic Courthouse
Washington County Historical Society
Washington County Library System
Washington County Public Affairs Office
White Bear Lake Historical Society
Wisconsin Regional Archives, University of Wisconsin-River Falls
Woodbury Heritage Society

Table of Contents

Table of Maps

Foreword

Improving transportation was one of Minnesota Territory's greatest needs. Leaders of the sparsely populated area realized that it was isolated in terms of both time and space from the nation's cultural and economic centers—Philadelphia, New York and Boston. They desperately wanted to stimulate settlement and create a prosperous modern society replete with all of the amenities of the East. The height of ambition for many pioneer Minnesotans was for their land to become the "New England of the West." To achieve this lofty goal they publicized Minnesota's allegedly salubrious climate, agricultural potential, prospective commerce, natural resources, water power, scenery and emigration routes.

Luring settlers to a territory commonly perceived as "An American Siberia" was challenging. Minnesota promoters always felt obliged to emphasize that St. Paul, their capital, was the practical head of navigation on the Mississippi River. Thus, Minnesota could be reached by traveling on one of nature's greatest highways.

Fortunately for Minnesota, the creation of the territory in 1849 coincided with an ongoing "transportation revolution" in the United States. The territory was started thirty-eight years after the first steamboat was navigated on the Mississippi and only nineteen years after the opening of the country's first railroad. The steamboat and railroad jolted the nation into an age of unprecedented speed. To impatient Americans, who earnestly believed the axiom that time was money, these new ways of moving people and goods assured the future greatness of the country they often fondly called "Young America."

Steamboating, which became commonplace on the Ohio and Mississippi rivers during the 1820s, was enthusiastically welcomed by emigrants and businessmen. But they soon found that steamboats were costly, seasonal, hazardous and subject to mechanical failures. The most spectacular losses of life were caused by fires and boiler explosions. Heavy newspaper coverage of these disasters caused public calls for federal government regulation of the steamboats and railroad construction. By the mid-1830s residents of the Mississippi River valley were longing for railroads, which would be both faster and safer than steamboats.

National consciousness about developing railroads was stimulated by the rapid growth of the United States in the 1840s. In a few years the country was greatly enlarged by the annexation of Texas, the settlement of the Oregon boundary dispute with Great Britain and the acquisition of the southwest as a result of war with Mexico. Binding sections together with railroads gained a sense of national urgency after the California gold rush started in 1840. In 1853 the federal government sponsored surveys of four possible transcontinental railroad routes, with the northernmost one running form St. Paul to Puget Sound.

The St. Paul–Puget Sound survey placed Minnesota in a new national perspective. Minnesota's boosters, looking both east and west, claimed that St. Paul, about equidistant from the Atlantic to the Pacific, was destined to become a great transportation hub. With an "all roads lead to Rome" mentality, they assumed their capital would become the metropolis of central North America. Their hopes for Minnesota's future greatness helps explain their warm reception of the Grand Excursion of 1854.

The steamboat excursion from Rock Island to St. Paul was the greatest single promotional event in the history of Minnesota Territory. By using each other, the proprietors of the Chicago and Rock Island Railroad and Minnesota officials publicized the linkage of the East and the Mississippi River, the scenic splendor of the Upper Mississippi and Minnesota's commercial promise. For those skeptical of some of the puffery associated with Minnesota boosterism, the railroad represented tangible proof of progress. Its reality brought Minnesota closer to the rest of the country. But the excursion also symbolized the transition into a new age, in which Minnesota would be liberated from frozen rivers and long winters without commercial ties with the East.

This fine work by Nancy and Robert Goodman is fitting for the observance of the grand excursion sesquicentennial. Through diligent research and lucid writing, the Goodmans skillfully describe the steamboat background of the grand excursion. In their chapters and sketches of numerous steamboats they show the vital role steamboats played in Minnesota's development. But by also portraying the nature and limitations of steamboating, they explain the attractiveness of railroads and the impact of publicity resulting from the grand excursion. The Goodmans ably describe the essential role of new technology in transportation that vaulted Minnesota and the rest of the nation into an increasingly industrialized world.

William E. Lass,
Professor Emeritus of History
Minnesota State University, Mankato

Mississippi riverboats at the St. Paul levee c. 1856. From left to right, they are the **Grey Eagle, Frank Steele, Jeannette Roberts** and **Time and Tide.** Photo Minnesota Historical Society.

CHAPTER ONE

The Grand Excursion of 1854

O ne hundred and fifty years ago, the rivers were America's highways and steamboats carried the traffic. Riverboats on the Mississippi and its tributaries connected Pittsburgh with Kansas City and St. Paul with New Orleans. In a time when land travel was difficult, time-consuming and expensive, the network of waterways and the paddlewheel steamer made the rapid settlement of the United States west of the Appalachians possible.

America's first railroads were built to give places in the hinterlands access to rivers and canals. Where there was a waterway, railroads were thought to be unnecessary. Many railroads were short, unconnected lines. In 1851 Chicago did not even have a rail connection with the eastern United States. To reach the city from New York you traveled by rail to New Buffalo on Lake Michigan then sailed across the lake to Chicago, a trip that took more than two weeks. Railroads were still considered to be wild speculations and it was difficult to raise capital to build western roads.

Chicago, after all, had access to Mississippi River markets via the Illinois and Michigan Canal, constructed in 1848 to unite the great lake port with the Illinois River. When a railroad

Railroads to Chicago c.1855. Chicago was first connected by rail to the East in 1852. At the time of the Grand Excursion, the line to Rock Island had been open less than three months. This map, published in 1856, confidently shows several routes not yet completed. From *Lloyd's Steamboat Directory and Disasters on the Western Waters.*

from Rock Island to the Illinois River port of La Salle was first proposed, it was meant to be a mere extension of the canal. People who contemplated railroads paralleling a canal were thought to be "visionaries."

Visionary Railroad Builders

Two such visionaries were engineer Henry Farnam and capitalist Joseph R. Sheffield, who had built several successful canals and railroads in the eastern United States. In 1852 they completed the Michigan Southern Railroad, the first to enter Chicago. When the first locomotive from the east chugged into Chicago that year it triggered a huge boom in trade, passengers and real estate values. Suddenly the trip to New York could be made in less than two days! Chicago was in a whirl of excitement.

Over objections from Illinois Canal interests, Farnam and Sheffield were given the contract to build the proposed Rock Island railroad, not merely from Rock Island to La Salle, but all the way from the Mississippi River to Chicago. Work began at once, and the first train from Chicago reached the Mississippi over the Chicago and Rock Island Railroad in February 1854. Even before the Rock Island Line was complete, it was carrying twice the traffic the promoters had planned for it and extra locomotives had been ordered.

The Atlantic Is Connected to the Mississippi!

Two celebrations were held to commemorate Sheffield and Farnam's great achievement of connecting the Atlantic seaboard with the Mississippi River. The first was a local festivity hosted by the city of Rock Island. On February 22, 1854, guests were taken on a rail excursion from Chicago to Rock Island and treated to a parade, banquet, entertainment and fireworks. The elegant dinner, which included thirteen toasts, was a temperance event. The festive party was put up in Rock Island overnight and returned to Chicago the next day, the 180-mile return trip taking seven hours and thirty minutes. While this all-expenses-paid excursion was confined to local guests, the enthusiasm that greeted it was not lost on the partners.

Farnam and Sheffield were eastern men, and both were very much aware of the general

Chicago, shown here in a birds-eye view from 1854, was a city of 70,000, notable for its planked roads (timber being cheaper than bricks) and a go-ahead attitude. Rock Island, Illinois had a population of about 4,500 and its sister city across the river, Davenport, Iowa was slightly larger, about 7,000. The largest city on the Upper Mississippi was Galena, Illinois, with a population of nearly 10,000. Detail of lithograph by Edward Mendel c.1854, Chicago Historical Society.

A Partial List of Notables on the Great Excursion

Millard Fillmore, ex-president
Roger Baldwin, governor of Connecticut
Joel Aldrich Matteson, governor of Illinois
John S. Barry, governor of Michigan
George Babcock, Boston historian
N. K. Hall, New York
Edward Bates, Missouri
General John Granger
Elbridge Gerry and the Misses Gerry,
    New York
Rev. Dr. Bacon, New Haven, CT
Thurlow Weed, *Albany Journal*
Epes Sargent, *Boston Transcript*
Charles A. Dana, *New York Tribune*
Charles Hale, *Boston Advertiser*
Hiram Fuller, *New York Mirror*
C. Cather Flint, *Chicago Tribune*
James F. Babcock, *New Haven Palladium*
Samuel Bowles, *Springfield Republican*
Judge J. C. McCurdy and daughter, CT
Colonel William Davenport, Philadelphia
William Higgins, Liverpool, England
Catherine M. Sedgwick, writer
Benjamin Silliman, professor at Yale
Judge Parker, law professor, Harvard
Henry Hubbard, professor at Dartmouth
J. F. Kennett, New York artist
W. Chauncey, ex-mayor of New York
Samuel J. Tilden, New York
Henry Farnam, Rock Island RR
Colonel Mix, Rock Island RR
Francis P. Blair Jr., St. Louis

ignorance that prevailed in the East about the New West and its potential. It occurred to them to invite some of their influential eastern friends on a six-day excursion. They would take them not only over the new rail line but also up the Mississippi River to St. Paul so that "they might see with their own eyes the resources of the New West." When word got out, requests for invitations poured in in such numbers that what was supposed to be a small party of friends turned into a great throng that crowded six Mississippi steamboats.

Excursion ticket

The Great Western Railroad Excursion Takes Shape

In early June guests of the railroad began arriving in Chicago and were lodged at the Tremont House. The press called the party "the most brilliant ever assembled," and the guests "the elite of the American Republic." Among the notables were lawyers and judges, doctors and divines, university professors, painters, poets, authors and historians—the leading lights of New York, Boston, New Haven (Farnam's home town) and Chicago. A host of political bigwigs

War Eagle, lead boat in the Grand Excursion, is shown a few years later loaded to the texas roof with excursionists. Photo Murphy Library, University of Wisconsin–La Crosse.

included Ex-president Millard Fillmore and the governors of Illinois, Michigan and Connecticut. Almost every eastern big-city newspaper sent a representative to write up the "Great Western Excursion." Many invited guests brought along their entire families, swelling the total of excursionists—invited and uninvited—to more than 1,200.

More Steamboats Are Needed!

Two trains of nine cars each left Chicago at 8:30 Monday morning, June 5, 1854, with about a thousand people aboard. Hundreds more joined the trains en route or met the excursion at Rock Island. When the trains arrived at the terminal at about 4 p.m., five of the best boats and most popular captains on the river were waiting. They were the Galena packets *Galena,* Captain D. B. Morehouse, and *War Eagle,* Captain D. S. Harris; and the St. Louis packets *Lady Franklin,* Captain LeGrande Morehouse, *G. W. Sparhawk,* Captain Monroeville Green, and *Golden Era,* Captain Hiram Bersie.

Three of these first-class riverboats had been added by the railroad promoters when it became obvious that there were twice as many people anxious to board as they had originally ticketed. Even so, the boats were quickly jammed, and possibly as many as a third of the excursionists elected to return to Chicago or continue on other boats to St. Louis rather than sleep on the cabin floor. Others agreed to a shorter outing, so the steamer *Jenny Lind* was hired at the last minute to take the extra passengers with the flotilla as far as Galena. At least 1,000 tourists made the full trip.

Facsimile of the bill of fare for one meal served on the steamboat *Galena* during the Excursion, copied in the St. Paul *Weekly Minnesotian* June 9, 1854.

Some accounts indicate that there were seven boats, the last being either the *Black Hawk* or *Black Warrior*, but company records show only six were hired, and of these, the newspapers agreed, five reached St. Paul. The Minnesota River steamer *Black Hawk,* which frequently made trips to St. Louis or Rock Island, could not have been involved—St. Paul newspapers noted her departure the morning of June 6 for Traverse des Sioux on the Minnesota River. No upper river steamer named *Black Warrior* is documented. However, given the daily traffic on the river, it is quite likely other packets did join those that had been chartered by Farnam for at least part of the way, adding to the grand parade, even if not a part of the official excursion.

"A Festival from Beginning to End"

At 7 p.m. Monday evening, after a "sumptuous feast" on the boats, the party put over to Davenport, Iowa, where speeches were made (including two by Millard Fillmore promoting U.S. internal improvements and the Great West). The evening concluded with fireworks shot off from Fort Armstrong across the Mississippi as the boats, wreathed with prairie flowers and evergreens, their brass bands playing, started up the river single file, led by Captain Smith Harris's *War Eagle.* The luxurious *Golden Era,* pride of the Galena Packet Company, with the Farnam family and the former president aboard, brought up the rear.

BILL OF FARE
ON BOARD THE
Steamer Galena
D. B. MOREHOUSE, MASTER.

June 9, ... 1854

SOUP.

Green Turtle,		
Oyster,		Clam.

FISH.

Baked Salmon,		Baked Pike,
White Fish,		" Pickerel.
	Mackinaw Trout.	

BOILED.

Game,		Corned Beef,
Tongue,		Chicken, egg sauce.
Turkey,		oyster sauce.

ROAST.

Beef,	Mutton,	Chickens,
Pork,	Veal,	Ducks
Pig,	Turkey,	Lamb.

GAME.

Prairie Chickens,	Snipe,
Buffalo Steak,	Quails.

ENTREES.

Oyster Pie — Chicken Pie — Brazed Fillet of Mutton — Boiled Chickens — Truffle of Fowl, wine sauce — Broiled Brook Trout.

PUDDINGS AND PASTRY.

PIES — Cranberry. Rhubarb. Currant. Cocoanut. Lemon. Tapioca.

DESSERT.

Raisins and Kisses,	Figs,
Almonds,	Prunes,
Pecan Nuts,	Filberts,
Oranges,	Pine apples

JELLIES, &c.

Calf's Foot,	Blanc Mange,
Madeira,	Charlotte Russe.

ICE CREAM.

Lemon,	Sherry,	Orange.

Dawn on Tuesday found the fleet a few miles below Bellevue, Iowa. As they neared Galena, Illinois—the upper river's biggest shipping port despite being nine miles from the Mississippi on the Fever River—the fleet was greeted with firing of artillery and waving of white handkerchiefs from every window. Carriages waited to drive the party out to visit the lead mines and enjoy a picnic in the woods. Then the passengers were off to a gala reception at Dubuque, Iowa, where not even a driving rainstorm could dampen the "booster" speeches. Next morning the boats stopped briefly at La Crosse, where despite continuing rain an enthusiastic crowd assembled to greet the flotilla; then it was on to St. Paul.

During daylight hours, watching the magnificent scenery glide by was the chief pastime of the passengers. Catherine Sedgwick on board the *Lady Franklin* even went so far as to compare the Mississippi favorably to the Rhine. The boats stopped several times a day to "wood up" allowing the excursionists to troop ashore. While they were wooding at Trempeauleau, Wisconsin, Miss Fillmore borrowed a horse and rode to the top of the bluff. A salvo of steamboat whistles greeted her appearance at the summit. In the evening the boats were tied together so passengers could visit freely. When the flotilla reached Lake Pepin, on Wednesday evening, four of the boats were lashed together to proceed up the lake side by side in the moonlight. Each boat had a band, which enabled the passengers to add "dancing, music, flirtations, et cetera" to their pursuits.

St. Paul in the early 1850s was a rapidly growing river town. The domed building at the rear is the territorial capitol. Lithograph from J. W. Bond, *Minnesota and Its Resources*, 1853.

Creature comforts were "munificently" provided for and, the passengers agreed (except, perhaps, for the gentlemen who were obliged to sleep on the floors and tables), would have done honor to first class hotels. Hunters and fishermen had been sent on ahead to procure game and fresh fish for the tables. Lobsters and oysters (brought in cans, of course) were served daily. West Indies pineapples and other fruits had been rushed upstream by Mississippi steamers, to arrive fresh at Rock Island only four days from the Caribbean. Live ducks and geese were carried in crates on the main deck, along with cows that provided fresh milk.

One steamer's kitchen produced the main courses, while another was given over entirely to making confections and desserts. Miss Sedgwick was astounded: "By what magic art such ices, jellies, cakes and pyramids veiled in showers of candied sugar were compounded in . . . a steamer's kitchen is a mystery yet to be settled," she wrote to a friend (who had returned back east for fear of crowding, or perhaps starving). She called the excursion "a festival from beginning to end."

St. Paul Caught by Surprise

By some unaccountable error of management, the boats arrived at St. Paul on Thursday morning, June 8, a day before they were expected. Nonetheless, as the boats rounded the bend into St. Paul, streamers flying and brass bands playing, the citizens rose to the occasion. St. Paul, then a settlement for only about a dozen years with a population of less than 5,000, had

A Motley Cavalcade Lands at St. Paul

All is bustle and confusion on shore and all sorts of vehicles are coming down the bank. There sit Governor Baldwin and Mrs. B. in high backed chairs in a long lumber wagon. There, in just such a wagon, sit Mr. McCurdy and daughter, surrounded by other ladies and gentlemen. There are Judge J. O. Phelps, C. B. Lines and Mr. Woodward of the *Journal* in a very handsome one-horse buggy. They have not waited for the uncertain movements of the committee, but have been to a stable and provided for themselves. . . . A St. Paul man told us to get a seat where we could! . . . Here is room, said Prof. Twining, come up here. We were soon on the vehicle and took position between Governor Berrie [sic], of Michigan, and Mr. Twining. On the seat below was Mr. Bancroft, the historian, his son and the driver of the carriage, and back of all was stretched out one of the editors of the New York *Times*.

James F. Babcock, *New Haven Palladium*, June 1854.

few attractions in itself. But Minnesota boasted one great sight, the Falls of St. Anthony, about nine miles distant. Welcoming speeches were forgotten as St. Paulites rushed to the landing with every available vehicle (including a one-horse water cart on which three editors mounted) to carry the visitors to the falls. In high spirits the party set off across the prairie to the little

Minnesota when it was the "wild west." The spectacular Falls of St. Anthony was a must-see item for tourists to Minnesota. Lithograph from J. W. Bond, *Minnesota and Its Resources,* 1853.

village of St. Anthony, now part of Minneapolis, to see the great wonder of the west. Crossing over to Nicollet Island, in the midst of the falls, the tourists performed a little ceremony of pouring water brought from the Atlantic Ocean into the stream, thus symbolically mingling the waters of East and West.

After a morning viewing the scenery, the excursionists returned to St. Paul and boarded their boats again for a short trip further up the Mississippi to Fort Snelling, about seven miles above St. Paul, stopping en route at Fountain Cave. Carriages took them to Lake Calhoun and Minnehaha Falls (which one bemused easterner pronounced "demnition fine").

That evening a reception for the visitors was held in the Territorial Capitol. Rooms were set aside for speeches and refreshments and a grand ball was held in the legislative hall. "The ladies of the party, and the ladies of St. Paul, are in full dress and the scene more resembles one often observed in the saloons of New York than one which could have been anticipated in any place in this new Territory," wrote one impressed editor.

During the speech making that evening, the former president declared the excursion one for which "history had no parallel, and such as no prince could possibly undertake." He went on to thrill St. Paulites by outlining the importance of connecting the Pacific coast with the Eastern states via a transcontinental railroad, and noting the important position St. Paul might assume as a central point on one of the routes.

The dancing broke up at eleven o'clock so the tourists could return to the landing where their boats lay illuminated, with steam hissing from their boilers. Just after midnight on June 9 the fleet cast off, and by Saturday morning, June 10, they were back at Rock Island. There the party disbanded, some returning east and others continuing on to St. Louis and other western points.

A Costly Venture That Paid Off Admirably

So well satisfied were the guests with the trip, the boats and their captains, that on every craft in the fleet a meeting was held among the passengers to pass resolutions expressing their thanks, and collections were taken to procure testimonial plates, pitchers, rings and other tokens of esteem to present to each boat's officers.

More than forty editors returned to their newspapers and magazines to wax eloquent on the beauties and riches of the West, and to urge travelers to follow them in making a "fashionable tour" on the mighty Mississippi to the magnificent Falls of St. Anthony.

The bill for the excursion, paid half by the Rock Island Railroad Company and half by Sheffield and Farnam, was reported to have been $50,000 (more than a million in today's money), so lavish were the accommodations. None of the passengers paid a dime for any transportation or the trip itself. The excursion had been conceived not so much as a pleasure trip as a way to make a thousand wealthy and influential people acquainted with the beauty, the resources and the prosperity of the Great West. By letting their influential friends "see the elephant" firsthand, Sheffield and Farnam hoped to remove the suspicions that easterners had of western railroads and all other western investments and induce them to put their money in western development.

They succeeded admirably. Crowed Fitch of the *Chicago Tribune,* "Should no one of the party invest a dollar in western enterprises, the testimony which they will be constrained to give in favor of western lands, western roads, western rivers and western products must and will tell favorably upon our future."

The spectacular public relations stunt paid off manyfold. Over the next few years visitors by the thousands landed at St. Paul, some anxious to see the sights, some prepared to make new homes in the West. Many were drawn not only by the glowing testimonials of the excursionists, but by the rail connections that made reaching the Mississippi River so easy and comfortable and by the commodious paddle steamboats that effortlessly carried them onward.

The New View from New York

Perhaps you have beheld such sublimity in dreams, but surely never in daylight waking elsewhere in this wonderful world. Over one hundred and fifty miles of unimaginable fairy-land, genie-land, and world of visions, have we passed during the last twenty-four hours . . . . Throw away your guide books; heed not the statement of travelers; deal not with seekers after and retailers of the picturesque; believe no man, but see for your-self the Mississippi River above Dubuque.

New York Times, June 20, 1854

CHAPTER TWO

What Changed in 1854?

The Grand Excursion of 1854 was the beginning of boom times in the Upper Mississippi Valley. The interest generated by this one six-day event led to an immediate increase in vacationers and immigrants making the voyage to St. Paul and other river towns. Favorable editorials in eastern newspapers helped attract investors to the west, especially to the railroads.

High Times on the Mississippi

Between 1854 and 1859 four more railroads were completed from the lake ports of Chicago and Milwaukee to the Upper Mississippi at Fulton, Dunleith, Prairie du Chien and La Crosse. As each line reached the river it connected with steamboats that carried passengers and freight on to river towns above or below. Railroads made travel from the eastern states

View of Dubuque, Iowa, c.1855, drawn by Lucinda Farnham. In June of 1855 the Illinois Central Railroad reached Dunleith, across the Mississippi River from Dubuque, spurring a great increase in river traffic that carried goods on from the railhead. Galena, several miles inland on the Fever River, began to lose its advantage as a shipping point from that time. Lithograph Dubuque Historical Society.

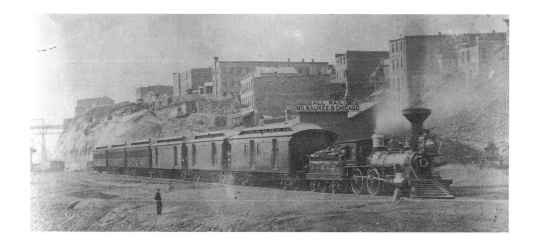

Rail had reached the Mississippi at La Crosse by 1858. It took nearly ten years longer, the Civil War intervening, for rail service from the east to reach St. Paul. Pictured is a Milwaukee and St. Paul engine and cars on the St. Paul levee about 1868. The bluff on which St. Paul was built is very evident. Minnesota Historical Society.

much easier and faster, and the regular flow of rail traffic led to unequaled steamboat service.

Customers flocked to the riverboats. Steamboat arrivals at the port of St. Paul jumped from 235 in the 1853 season to 1,026 by 1857 and the population of Minnesota Territory skyrocketed, tripling in less than three years—from under 50,000 in 1854 to over 150,000 by 1857. St. Paul packet companies estimated that during the thirty-or-so-week season of 1855 alone they brought 30,000 immigrants into Minnesota. River cities in Wisconsin and Iowa also saw tremendous gains during these years as they channeled newcomers to their backcountry.

Steamboats on the Defensive

It was an illusory bonanza, because all advantages lay with the railroads. Riverboats had geographic limitations, and much of the Upper Mississippi river system was not navigable by larger boats and in all seasons. On average,

railroad distances between two points on a river are shorter by one-third, so once railroads were built parallel to the Mississippi, distance and speed became major factors in the decline of steamboats. The railroads provided fast year-round service and reliability.

While the limitations of steamboat transportation did not matter when the upper river settlements were first developing and most commerce was next to the river, communities that were settled inland soon became dependent upon the railroads. At first boat rates were cheaper than rail by fifty percent, but in short order steamboat companies were forced to lower prices even more to remain competitive. By 1855 the Mississippi had been bridged and inevitably all-rail rates fell below rail-plus-river rates. By the end of the Civil War the struggle between the railroad and the steamboat had ceased. The railroads with their greater size and financial resources were able to cut out the steamers.

And so the Grand Excursion promotion of 1854, which marked the beginning of skyrocketing western expansion stimulated by railroad traffic, also foreshadowed the end of the packet steamboat on the Mississippi. After the brief steamboating boom, western expansion was carried increasingly by the railroads. By 1860 railroads had imposed a new geography on the western landscape; hamlets, towns and cities sprang up like magic on the rail lines. Packet boats flourished longest on the northern part of the river, where there was no rival north-south rail connection until after the Civil War. But once the railroads had caught up with the frontier, the steamboat's day was done.

Steamboats Pave the Way

Before the railroads were steamboats. If the steamboats had not pioneered the way the railroads could not have come in later years. The carriage of goods and produce by steamer, on the Mississippi and its tributaries, made possible a settlement of the country that later furnished traffic sufficient to support the railroads. . . .

The mere coming of the railroad did not harm the steamboat traffic; on the other hand it gave it a great stimulus. . . . The country, by that time considerably settled, began to produce grain and pork for the market, and if the steamboats did not carry it all the way they at least carried it to the most convenient railroad. Business boomed, and boats multiplied in those days. They were the days of good boats, and fast time, and fine meals, and prosperity; high wages for good rivermen, and grand dividends for the steamers that carried the traffic.

Then the railroads crossed the river; first here at Davenport, and later at other points above and below, and then the steamboat business began to fail and fall away.

Capt. W. H. Gabbert, *The Half-Century Democrat* (Davenport), Oct. 22, 1905

What This Book Is About

For forty years, between 1823 and the Civil War, steamboats dominated Upper Mississippi transportation and played a pivotal role in developing the vast Mississippi basin from a sparsely populated frontier to a well-populated area of great economic importance. In the opinion of historian Louis C. Hunter, "During the second quarter of the nineteenth century, the wheels of commerce in this extensive region were almost literally paddle wheels."

River steamboats helped hurry up settlement on the American frontier. Without them, development would have been slower, and the pattern of settlement different. Given the poor state of frontier roads, development in the west followed the rivers. Settlers took up land within a short wagon ride of the rivers and local market towns arose along those same rivers, served by the steamboats that brought the supplies they needed and carried their produce to market.

Chronicling the Rise and Fall of the Packet Boats

The steamboats in this book are mainly packet boats, that is, all-purpose passenger and freight carriers. Packets did whatever business there was to be done, which might include, in the years before boats were built specifically for rafting, towing log rafts through Lake St. Croix and Lake Pepin. Through the end of the Civil War packets did most of the work on the river.

After the coming of the railroads, boats began to specialize. Some became car ferries, transferring rail cars from shore to shore. Others were built as excursion boats, outfitted with ballrooms and salons. Some went to work for the government, clearing snags and dredging the commercial channels. There was a period of expansion as large sternwheelers came into their own as towboats moving bargeloads of produce to the railheads. And from the mid-1860s on, powerful raftboats became common on the Mississippi. But when this story ends, in 1854, these types were still in the future for the upper river.

Showboats were popular on the Lower Mississippi and Ohio rivers in the years before the Civil War, but no showboats are recorded as having come through to St. Paul during the 1823 to 1854 period. Show and circus boats, in any

The boatyard upstream from the port of Cincinnati in part of a panoramic view taken by daguerreotypists Charles Fontayne and William S. Porter in September 1848. This is the earliest known photograph showing river steamboats. While none of the visible boats is identifiable as an Upper Mississippi visitor, they are good examples of the types then working. Most early paddlewheel steamers were built on the Ohio River. Photo Public Library of Cincinnati and Hamilton County.

MAP OF
MISSISSIPPI RIVER
BETWEEN
ST LOUIS AND ST PAUL
TO ILLUSTRATE
OLD TIMES ON UPPER MISSISSIPPI
~ BY ~
GEO. B. MERRICK

case, were usually not self-propelled. Most were simply theaters floating on barges and were pushed by towboats.

Pictures of early steamboats are scarce. The earliest known photograph—a daguerreotype made of steamboats at the landing in Cincinnati—dates from 1848. Only if a boat survived into the age of photography could a picture be included in this book. However, many earlier steamboats were depicted in sketches, paintings and lithographs made by early travelers, and those that are identifiable have been included.

Narrowing the Focus to the Upper Mississippi

The Upper Mississippi is the part of the river above St. Louis. It really consists of three sections, differing in topography and climate, each of which developed in a different way.

The Lower Section

The lower river, from St. Louis to Keokuk, Iowa, was the first to attract settlers. With the settlements came daily packets, shuttling passengers and freight. Boats that came above St. Louis had to be powerful enough to stem the turbulent currents of the river, and so were often

Upper Mississippi and tributaries. Galena, center of the lead trade, was by far the busiest port above St. Louis. There was comparatively little river traffic north of Galena until the territories of Wisconsin, Iowa and Minnesota were formed (1836–1849) and treaties with the Indians created an abundance of cheap land and timber. Map from G. B. Merrick *Old Times on the Upper Mississippi*, 1937.

Paddlewheel steamers crowd the St. Louis levee during the riverboat's heyday. St. Louis was a great transshipping point, where boats such as **Amulet** (far right) from the Upper Mississippi met boats that regularly plied the Missouri, Ohio and Lower Mississippi Rivers. Photo c.1848, St. Louis Mercantile Library.

too large to venture north of Keokuk and risk their hulls on the Des Moines rapids. Small boats, unable to compete with the larger St. Louis packets, often worked only above Keokuk.

The Middle Section

The middle section, 225 miles from Keokuk to Galena, Illinois, was developed by and for the lead industry. From the eighteenth century on, flatboats loaded with lead had been floated down to St. Louis from Galena and Dubuque, Iowa. When the Black Hawk Purchase of 1832 secured the area for the United States, squatters poured into southwestern Wisconsin and northwestern Illinois. By 1836, more than 5,000 people—nearly one-half the population of Wisconsin Ter-ritory—lived in the lead district, headquartered at Galena. Steamboats, usually towing barges or flatboats, carried on the lead trade through the mid-1840s. Boats plying this stretch of river had to pass the two sets of rapids, at Rock Island and Keokuk, that for years constituted a huge physical barrier to navigation. Some steamboats plied only between the rapids, moving on cargo that had been put off at one end of the rapids and carried by flatboat or wagon to the other.

The lead freighters seldom ventured above Galena.

The Upper River

This book focuses on the northern third of the river, the 275-mile section between Galena and the Falls of St. Anthony (now Minneapolis). This stretch was last to develop, partly because of its brief navigation season and partly because there was little or no business to be done north of the lead mines. While extremely scenic, the upper river was narrow, winding and shallow, and filled with islands and sloughs through which the channel weaved back and forth depositing sandbars and cutting through banks. It was liable to low water and its settlements were cut off from the rest of the world for five or more months of the year because of the freeze up of the rivers. This part of the river and its navigable tributaries—the Wisconsin, Chippewa, St. Croix and Minnesota rivers—required a different kind of steamboat, built specifically for low water and maneuverability.

In the pages that follow the spotlight is turned on the paddlewheel boats that served the Mississippi River above Galena—there were more than 250 of them over the three decades before the railroads changed upper river commerce forever—and the significant part these steamers played in the development and settlement of the Upper Mississippi basin.

The winding channel of the northern Mississippi River presented a challenge to steamboat pilots. This view by Edwin Whitefield c. 1856 shows the river at Homer, near present Winona, Minnesota. Watercolor Minnesota Historical Society.

CHAPTER THREE

What Was a River Steamboat?

The paddlewheel steamboat was a unique form of transportation, designed for a particular function—the transportation of freight and passengers on America's inland rivers. The river steamboat came into being because of the particular circumstances that existed on the Mississippi and its tributaries in the early days of the nineteenth century. Just at the very moment that steam power was being developed, Americans were streaming into the continent's vast western lands. The need for transportation fueled development of the powered boat, and the ability of these boats to carry huge quantities of materials long distances very cheaply helped promote America's western expansion.

Types and Construction

The western steamboat was a specialized craft, designed for navigation on shallow, winding rivers. Light of draft, keelless, very lightly framed and very flexible, these boats could go where no ocean-going steamer or sailing vessel could navigate. Some, it was advertised, could "float on a heavy dew."

Although many people may think first of gambling casinos and showboats when they hear the word steamboat, during the period from the 1820s through 1854 nearly all riverboats, large and small, were versatile packets that carried both freight and passengers.

Hulls Evolve for River Travel

The earliest steam-powered boats had been heavy drafted—deep, blunt and round-bottomed with keels like sailing vessels. As steamboat design progressed, boats became shallower, narrower and longer. These modifications allowed them to carry full cargo on less water than earlier boats had needed with light loads. Many needed less than 18 inches of water to float. Their narrow, flat-bottomed hulls supported exceptionally wide decks, sometimes twice as wide as the hull, with flared extensions called guards that continued the deck out over the water. Guards evolved to protect the side paddlewheels from floating debris, but narrow ones were used even on sternwheel boats because they added so much cargo capacity and provided a handy walkway.

Typical sidewheeler

Most early Upper Mississippi boats were from 70 to 160 feet long and capable of carrying from 100 to 200 tons of freight, although by the end of the period larger boats began to appear. As there was no room in the shallow hold for the machinery, the boilers and engines were mounted right on the main deck, which was usually left open to allow easy loading of firewood and cargo.

Most boats, except the smallest, had a second deck called the boiler deck that often extended out over the guards to give protection to the main deck cargo. This deck held the main cabin and staterooms, and was topped with a hurricane roof (sometimes called hurricane deck) through which the main cabin skylight projected.

On bigger boats, built after the mid-1840s there was a third deck, called the texas, that supported the 12-foot square pilot house.

Topping it all off were the twin smokestacks, some as high as 90 feet above the waterline to assure that any sparks would burn out before they fell on the cargo. There were no bridges to contend with in the earliest days, but starting in the 1830s, when railroads began bridging the Ohio River, smokestacks were hinged and could be folded back to allow boats to pass under bridges in periods of high water.

Hulls were very long in proportion to their depth and width, with no keel and no beams to give stiffness. They were built on the model of a barge, with only a four- or five-foot deep hold.

The **Black Hawk** is a small sidewheel river packet from the 1850s. This low-water boat (she drew only 17 inches unloaded) was able to navigate the shallowest tributaries, such as the St. Croix and Minnesota rivers. Her shape, widest at the paddleboxes and tapering to the front, is typical. Flaring guards extended over the water to protect the paddlewheels, making the deck much wider than the hull. Photo Winona County Historical Society

Boats needing more than five feet of water were severely restricted in operating on western rivers that had a tendency to dry up in midsummer. Heavier boats also were unable to pass the two sets of rapids on the Mississippi, at Keokuk and Rock Island, which in many years carried less than four feet of water.

The long rake at the bow of a riverboat meant that the boat needed no wharf to tie up to—the pilot could make a shore landing almost anywhere. A landing stage at the front of the main deck could be swung out to load and unload passengers and cargo. Smaller boats without a crane simply pushed out a gangplank from boat to shore.

But the long, narrow hull also meant the boat had a tendency to "hog," that is, its ends would droop while the center rose. This was especially true of a larger boat with heavy machinery installed and a large cargo capacity. The problem was solved by development of the hog chain system of bracing the hull. The so-called chains were actually wrought iron rods 1–2½ inches in diameter installed on wooden poles or braces arranged so as to counteract the loads at the boilers and engines. They were especially prominent on sternwheelers, as they needed a

Typical of the smaller sternwheel river packets is the **Gardie Eastman.** Note the prominent hog chain framing system rising above the top deck that kept the boat straight. The sides of a sternwheeler are straighter, the guards smaller than on most sidewheelers. Wooden fenders along each side prevent damage from docks. Photo Winona County Historical Society.

very large truss to offset the weight of their single rear paddlewheel.

Sidewheelers and Sternwheelers

River steamers were propelled either by two side paddlewheels mounted amidships or by one large sternwheel. Both rigs had their uses and drawbacks. Hogging was easier to resist in sidewheelers because of the central placement of the engines and paddlewheels. Sidewheelers also were easier to maneuver, since the wheels could turn in opposite ways. However, the huge paddlewheels were exposed to floating debris and the wheelhouses took up a lot of deck room.

Sternwheel boats had steering problems. They were difficult to handle in high winds and their rudders, which were ahead of the wheel, were often ineffective. On tight river bends they had to stop and back and let the bow swing. But sternwheel boats weighed less, so they were more useful in shallow water, and the hull protected the buckets, or paddles. During the 1830s side-wheelers were favored, but by the 1840s, once the problem of supporting the heavy wheel was

Composition for Covering Boilers &cc.

Road scrapings, free from stones, 2 parts; cow manure, gathered from the pasture, 1 part; mix thoroughly, and add to each barrowful of the mixture 6 lbs. of fire clay; 1/2 lb. of flax shoves or chopped hay, and 4 oz. of teased hair. It must be well mixed and chopped; then add as much water as will bring to the consistency of mortar, the more it is worked the tougher it is.

From Alan L. Bates, *The Western Rivers Steamboat Cyclopoedium.*

solved with hog chains, sternwheelers came back. They had more pushing power, making them ideal for use as towboats and pushing log rafts. The real rafter, which was a towboat powerful enough to control a log raft in the Mississippi current, did not come into being until the late 1860s.

Paddlewheels, despite their weight, were admirably suited for river use. Although the screw propeller became available in the 1850s, it was seldom used on riverboats as it was not well adapted to shallow water, did not work well in reverse and was difficult to repair. Wheel arms and buckets suffered frequent damage from fixed and floating obstacles, but being mostly out of the water and made of wood, were easily repaired by the boat's carpenter. Timber was used for hulls and paddlewheels long after steel became available because of its ability to absorb shocks and its ease of repair.

Engines and Boilers

The first steamboats had low-pressure engines developed from stationary steam engines. They were severely underpowered, and soon high-pressure engines were developed. Most boats had two engines, one to a wheel on sidewheelers. Larger sternwheelers also had two engines to provide more even power to the wheel. The long connecting rod between piston and crank was called a pitman, and it, too, was usually made of wood for flexibility and ease of repair.

The boiler was horizontal with two internal flues, a firebox under one end and a riveted shell, the whole covered with an insulating material. Boats had from one to eight boilers, which stood forward on the main deck on support rods and facing the bow for draft. Because the raw river water used was so muddy, boilers had to be cleaned after every run and the mud scaled out by the engineer's helper. Some boats running on muddy tributaries had to clean their boilers several times a day.

All riverboats burned wood, although some may have used coal, resinous pine and other highly combustible materials. The desire to run "a hot boat" caused many a captain or engineer to compromise safety by dumping a barrel of waste fat into the firebox, letting the water level drop so as to carry a larger head of steam, and hanging weights on the safety valve. Flue collapses and boiler explosions were common, even on boats not being pushed to the limit. More prudent captains towed safety barges, which kept passengers and valuable cargo away from the chief danger.

On the Upper Mississippi many people living along the river kept wood yards to supply the boats. To save time on upriver trips, some of the fast packets loaded fuelwood from flatboats taken in tow, which were then released to drift back. Steamers burned 20 to 30 cords of wood a day—fuelwood accounted for about a third of a boat's running cost.

The Race for Light Weight and Fast Returns

Western river steamboats were very lightly built. To achieve the light draft that allowed them to operate on shallow rivers, every extra pound of weight had to be pared away. For this reason, and for cheap repairs, riverboats were made of wood, and lightweight wood at that. Hull timbers were small and a considerable part of the main deck was left unenclosed to reduce weight and make handling freight and fuel easier. The upper works were of flimsy construction, just strong enough to hold together, but this construction also minimized the topheaviness as decks rose higher and higher. It was partly to save weight that the large low-compression engines were done away with in favor of smaller high-pressure types and a battery of small boilers replaced one large one. The development of long, narrow hulls

> ## Even Light Draft Boats Have Troubles
>
> We used to have our troubles of navigation, get stuck on bars and have to spar or warp to get away, strike logs and stumps and snags, and all that. . . .
>
> It was low water that made the trouble. I have seen men wade the Mississippi many a time at places above [Davenport]. I remember one summer when the river almost ran dry, as it seemed, and the company sent me up to St. Paul to get a little 12-inch draft boat that had been built for local St. Paul trade. Just at the head of Lake Pepin, running in the dark, something appeared in the middle of the channel, dead ahead, and we stopped. Out of the darkness came a voice— "What'n the hell are you fellows trying to do?" We hadn't more than about 15 inches of water under us and we had pulled up just in time to miss running down a farmer and a load of hay, with which he was fording the channel between his home on the mainland, and the island on which he had cut his crop. Well—the people on the boat laughed some, if the farmer didn't.
>
> Capt. W. H. Gabbert, *The Half-Century Democrat* (Davenport), Oct. 22, 1905

let riverboats carry heavy loads on little water, and also gave them better speed, which allowed more trips in a season. The ideal, as one riverman put it, was a boat so built that "when the river is low and the sandbars come out for air, the first mate can tap a keg of beer and run the boat four miles on the suds."

Cost was a great consideration. The average life of an Upper Mississippi steamer was short, only four to five years on average, and the period a boat could be employed during any year varied with the depth of water and the time the river was ice-free, on the upper river usually only from May first through mid-November. Insurance rates for boats and cargo were high, and the construction presented a serious fire hazard. Most owners endeavored to keep their initial investment at a minimum and extend their season to the maximum. As a rule of thumb, a river steamer could be expected to earn back her initial cost in one accident-free season.

Traveling on a Paddlewheel River Steamer

In the heyday of the steam packet, a river trip could be quite an experience. Traveling on the *Ben Campbell* in 1852, a passenger (Elizabeth Ellet, *Summer Rambles in the West*) noted that the boat "rivaled in elegance the Lake and Ohio

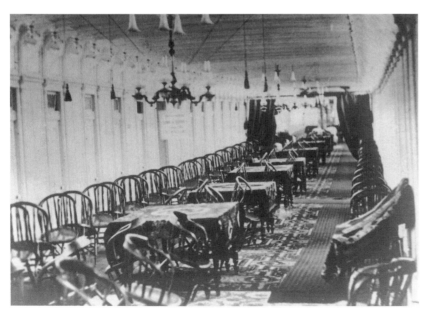

steamers; the staterooms were large . . . and the fare was so excellent that one was naturally at a loss to conceive how passengers could possibly be conveyed four hundred miles, lodged and fed sumptuously, and provided with attendance for four dollars each, less than one would have to pay at an ordinary hotel."

But on even the most elegant of boats, the main deck was a picture of pandemonium. Travelers stepped aboard from the landing stage onto the main deck, where wood and cargo were being loaded, animals stabled, and deck passengers with all their luggage staking out claims. Farm tools and machinery, seed corn, cast-iron stoves, kegs of nails and gristmills were carefully loaded onto the main deck; lighter items, such as chicken coops, chairs and buggies were often strapped to the roof. Seldom did any cargo go into the shallow hold. The hatches of the hold were small and apt to be covered by deck cargo and firewood. In the midst of it all were the gaping fireboxes being fed wood by sweating firemen as the engineers got up steam.

The second or boiler deck, supported by the framework of the paddleboxes and posts spaced at intervals, held the main cabin. This cabin, often called the salon, was lit by a clerestory of skylights and was as elegant, welcoming and comfortable as the owners could make it. It was often elaborately painted and furnished with carpets, mirrors, lamps, stoves, velvet sofas and comfortable chairs.

The main cabin of a passenger boat provided luxurious accommodations and the finest food. Staterooms opened off both sides. The ladies' salon was curtained off at the rear. Photo Murphy Library, University of Wisconsin–La Crosse.

Steamboat Terms

Boiler deck: The second deck.

Buckets: The paddles.

Guards: Extensions of the main deck out over the water.

Hog chain: Iron rod framing used to hold up the ends of the boat.

Hurricane roof or deck: The roof of the top, or boiler, deck

Pilothouse: The rooftop cabin where the boat is steered.

Salon or saloon: The main cabin.

Skylight: Windowed projection of the main cabin through the roof.

Stateroom: Individual cabin opening to the salon and the deck.

Texas deck: Crew's rooms on the skylight roof.

Wheelhouse: Protective casing around the side paddlewheel.

Parts of a River Steamboat

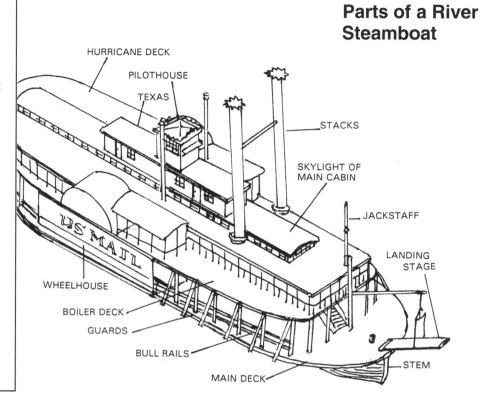

The salon also served as dining hall and the rear portion was reserved for the ladies' cabin. At the front was the gentlemen's cabin with bar and card tables and there also was the boat's business office.

On the earliest packets, passenger accommodations were only curtained berths on each side of the main cabin, but by the 1840s boats boasted two-bunk cabins with adjacent washrooms that opened both into the main cabin and onto the deck. Small toilet rooms were located against the paddle boxes on sidewheelers or at the stern on sternwheelers. Passengers were free to walk on the top roof, or hurricane deck, but usually could not do so without being covered with soot and sparks. This roof and the roof of the skylight were covered with fire-resistant canvas topped with paint and sand to thwart fires. The hurricane roof also had a high crown to shed rain and snow, so walking there was uncomfortable. The utilitarian main deck was enclosed with sturdy wooden bull railings, removable in sections for easier loading of cargo, but the top decks featured fancy railings with a lot of gingerbread trim, giving rise to the phrase, "Steamboat Gothic."

A small cabin on the skylight roof, called the texas, contained cabins for the captain and crew. Perched on the highest point at the front of the texas and often reachable only by ladder was the pilothouse, which until the invention of good window glass was open to the elements winter and summer and gave the pilot a 360-degree view. The pilothouse was the boat's nerve center. It connected the pilot, who was entirely responsible for the boat's course, to the captain and engine room via a speaking tube and a system of bells.

The ship's bell, not to be confused with the engine room signal bells, was mounted on the forward roof and used to signal the crew, sound fog warnings and announce the boat's arrivals and departures. By the mid-1850s, many boats had steam whistles.

Cabin Passage

For the cabin passenger, the steamboat was a remarkably swift and easy way to travel, compared to cramped and bone-jangling land transport, offering luxury otherwise unknown to the general public. Boat owners vied with each other to put out the choicest meats and pastries to gain passengers. They advertised such amenities as brass bands, dances, lectures, concerts and other diversions. For many passengers, the best entertainment was provided by the wild and rugged scenery, the opportunities for exploration when the boat stopped for wood, and the not infrequent impromptu races between boats.

However, since river steamers were very lightly built, their comfort level could be low. Even some cabin passengers found the luxury of the riverboat could not make up for its shortcomings. Passengers on the poorer class of boats complained of indigestible food, inadequate washing facilities, scanty bed clothes, leaky roofs and drafty cabins. Others found their fellow travelers an undesirable lot of drunkards, gamblers and backwoodsmen whose table manners showed a lamentable lack of restraint. Some captains, anxious to make as much as possible from each trip, crowded the boat beyond capacity with passengers and freight so that water washed over the guards. Even when the cabins were roomy, the passengers well behaved, and the meals excellent, the vibration from the engines and heat from the boilers could make life aboard intolerable. The less enthusiastic compared their boat to a "floating bathhouse" or even "hell afloat."

"Hell Afloat"

The expression of "Hell afloat" ought to be reserved for a small high-pressure steamboat in the summer months in America; the sun darting his fierce rays down upon the roof above you, which is only half-inch plank, and rendering it so hot that you quickly remove your hand if, by chance, you put it there; the deck beneath your feet so heated by the furnaces below that you cannot walk with slippers; you are panting and exhausted between these two fires, without a breath of air to cool your forehead. Go forward, and the chimneys radiate a heat which is even more intolerable. Go—but there is nowhere to go, except overboard, and then you lose your passage.

Frederick Marryat, *A Diary in America*, 1837

Deck Passage

Deck passengers, who often worked as wooders for a reduced fare, were without the accommodations enjoyed by cabin passengers. Crowded onto the exposed lower deck they had to provide their own bedding and meals, often cooking on the deck. The more freight was taken on board, the less room there was for the deck passengers, who usually outnumbered the cabin passengers by four to one. The conditions were not unlike those experienced by steerage passengers on the immigrant ships of the period. When livestock was on board, deckers lived with the smell.

Given the unsanitary conditions, it is not surprising that many boats arrived at upper river ports with dozens of sick and dying passengers, mostly to be found among those on deck. Deck passengers, and members of the crew who shared their quarters, also suffered the most accidents. There was little to protect them when boilers exploded, and as the main deck was often not far above water in cases of collision drownings were common.

A Travel Revolution

Economy of travel on river steamers more than made up for their dangers and discomforts in the minds of many passengers. Overland travel cost substantially more and subjected the traveler

Deck passengers at rest. Families slept where they could amidst the freight on the main deck in conditions that were dirty and uncomfortable and often promoted the spread of contagious diseases such as cholera. Drawing from *Lloyd's Steamboat Directory and Disasters on The Western Waters*, 1856

to terrifying roads, frequent breakdowns and overturns and often abominable accommodations. On the whole, travel by stagecoach was deemed even more dangerous than travel by river steamer in the west. The boiler deck of the better class of boat was easily the equal in comfort of a first-class hotel and the meals were included! To the general traveling public the steamboat represented a revolution in travel accommodations, a wonderfully swift and comfortable, even luxurious, way to get to one's destination.

CHAPTER FOUR

Early History of River Steamboats

Whatever their drawbacks, river steamboats represented a transportation revolution. Before the coming of the paddlewheel steamer, passengers and cargo were moved upriver solely by human or animal muscle power. Only small cargoes could be taken in Indian canoes and rowboats called bateaux.

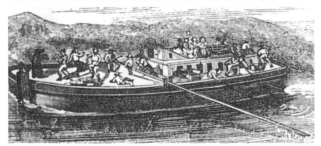

Flatboat, sometimes called a broadhorn for its long sweep oars. Drawing from *Lloyd's Steamboat Directory and Disasters on the Western Waters,* 1856.

Flatboats and barges, the earliest pioneers' riverboats, were generally built and loaded upriver and floated down to New Orleans where they were sold for their lumber along with the produce they carried. They were steered by oars, needed rather deep water and were almost impossible to move upstream. The crews walked or rode a mule back to their homes.

THE KEEL-BOAT.

Keelboat being poled. Drawing Winona County Historical Society.

Keelboats were an improvement, moving upstream at an average of two miles per hour and downstream at upwards of twelve miles an hour. These sleek 20- to 40-ton shallow draft boats were usually propelled by poling. They had a gangway on either side so crewmen could set their poles and walk to the stern, thus moving the craft forward. They could also be sailed, cordelled (dragged from shore) or warped (winched by a rope taken ahead and fixed on shore). In high water the crew might move them by bushwhacking—pulling them along on the trees and bushes.

Keelboats took a month to travel downriver from Cincinnati to New Orleans, and more than four months for the return trip. The earliest steamboats could manage the trip down in twelve days and upstream in thirty-six.

Invention of the River Steamboat

The new era in American transportation dawned in 1807 when Robert Fulton demonstrated the first practical steam-powered vessel. His novel craft, the *Clermont,* described by one eye-witness as a "backwoods saw-mill mounted on a scow and set on fire," amazed many skeptics when it steamed up the Hudson River to Albany, covering 150 miles in thirty-two hours. But western rivers and western distances presented greater hurdles. St. Louis was ten times as far from New Orleans as Albany was from New York, and the Mississippi current was three times as strong as the Hudson.

In the spring of 1810, Nicholas Roosevelt (a great grand-uncle of future United States presi-

dent Teddy) established a boatyard in Pittsburgh and began constructing a steamboat according to plans furnished by his partner, Robert Fulton. In October 1811 the *New Orleans* began her maiden voyage. The pioneer steamboat of the Mississippi Valley was a sidewheeler of 370 tons (the tonnage of a boat is a calculation of cubic capacity). She carried her freight in the bow, her engines and smokestacks were exposed amidships and her rear cabin was divided into two sections. She also carried two masts equipped with sails, which turned out to be useful. Surviving North America's worst earthquake (centered near the Mississippi at New Madrid, Missouri, during which the Mississippi actually

To celebrate the centennial of western steamboat navigation, this replica of the 1811 **New Orleans** was built and paraded in 1911. Photo Winona County Historical Society.

The Upper Mississippi in 1820

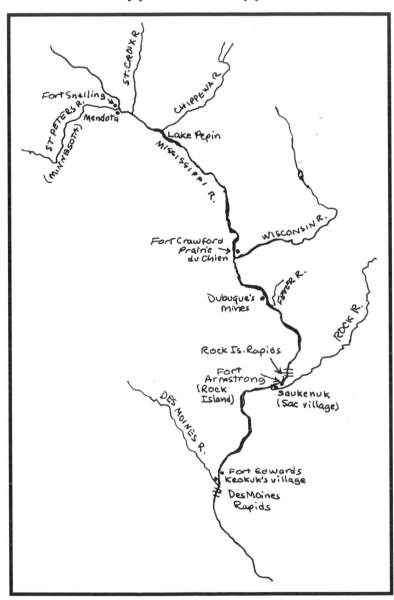

ran backwards), fire in her forward cabin, and the breaking of one paddlewheel, the *New Orleans* finally arrived at the port for which she was named eighty-two days out of Pittsburgh. Her deep V-shaped hull and low-pressure engine prevented her from being really suited to the mighty Mississippi: the best she could do was travel the more placid lower river from New Orleans to Natchez.

Henry Shreve Builds a Practical Riverboat

While half a dozen steamboats were built in the next three to four years, all were simply keelboats with engine and boilers dumped in the hold. They drew six to ten feet of water and their low-pressure engines did not provide enough power. It was left to Captain Henry Shreve to develop the pattern that all later Mississippi riverboats were to follow. He built his *Washington* on a flatboat, put the boiler and high-pressure engine on the main deck and built another deck over that, topping it off with a pilothouse.

The 400-ton *Washington,* largest boat and first two-decker on western waters, left Louisville, Kentucky, in the summer of 1816, steamed down the Ohio and Mississippi rivers to New Orleans and returned to Louisville—in just forty-five days! This boat removed all doubt that steam travel was practical on western rivers, and it proved to be the best design for upstream navigation on the Mississippi. Forty years later, the *Eclipse,* built to the same plan and at 1,117 tons the largest side paddlewheel riverboat ever built, made the trip from New Orleans to Louisville in four days and nine hours.

Steam powered boats gave new momentum to the growth of the great American West and the settling of the Mississippi River valley. Without the steamboat, the rapid rise of such western cities as Dubuque, La Crosse and St. Paul would be unthinkable.

Soldiers and Miners Draw Steamboats to the Upper Mississippi

At first there was little reason for boats to attempt travel on the upper Mississippi north of St. Louis because there was no business to be done there. However, in the early years of the century, miners began digging lead from the hillsides of what is now eastern Iowa, northwestern Illinois and southwestern Wisconsin. In 1816 the first flatboats loaded with galena (lead) ore were floated down to St. Louis. And in 1818 the United States War Department sent troops into the wilderness of what is now Minnesota to build a frontier post at the mouth of the St. Peters (now Minnesota) River, which was soon named Fort Snelling. Other frontier forts were located on the Mississippi at Prairie du Chien, Wisconsin, and Rock Island, Illinois, and all were supplied from downriver by keelboats and bateaux.

As a profitable commerce began in lead ore, miners and military supplies a better means of transportation was called for.

Zebulon Pike First Paddle Steamer at St. Louis

In August 1817 the first steamboat reached St. Louis from downriver. She was the *Zebulon M. Pike,* at 31 tons the next-to-smallest steamboat ever recorded on the Mississippi, with a low-pressure engine that rendered her so underpowered her crew often resorted to poling her like a keelboat. However, this little "batwing" boat (the term applied to a steamer with no paddleboxes to cover her sidewheels), was greeted with cheers at St. Louis for her feat of connecting the upper river with gulf and Ohio River ports.

Once the door to river commerce was opened, other boats began to ply the Upper Mississippi. The *Constitution* arrived at St. Louis that October, and several boats the following year. During 1818 and 1819 over sixty boats were built for western river trade, and St. Louis quickly became a great commercial hub, docking boats at her levee from the Ohio, Missouri and Mississippi rivers and even ocean-going vessels from New Orleans.

Still, it was six years before a steamboat would be able to take on the challenges of the Upper Mississippi. The river above St. Louis was wide but shallow, often no more than three feet deep. The channel was subject to shifting and cutting, producing new sandbars and islands overnight and as quickly making old ones disappear. The two sets of rapids, at the mouth of the Des Moines River and above Rock Island, remained challenges to steamboat pilots for many years. At first, steamboats were too underpowered to run these rapids upstream.

Travelers and their luggage were put off at one end of the rapids and transferred in wagons or carriages some twenty miles to the other end where the time-consuming process would be repeated and they would embark again on another boat.

Virginia Steams to Fort Snelling

In May 1823 the first boat to cross both rapids of the Mississippi arrived at Fort Snelling. The *Virginia* was a sidewheeler, 118 feet long and 109 tons, requiring a good stage of water. Among the passengers were the Italian explorer Giacomo Beltrami and Lawrence Taliaferro, the Indian Agent. *Virginia* was almost rebuffed by the Des Moines rapids, but a second try after lightening her load carried her through. On her ascent of the longer Rock Island rapids, she struck a rock, but fortunately a rising river helped her over.

Her progress was slow as she proceeded cautiously where no steamboat had gone before, striking five sandbars and taking five days to

Fort Snelling is perched dramatically on the cliffs overlooking both the Mississippi and Minnesota rivers. This detail from a watercolor painted by John Caspar Wild in 1844 shows a steamboat approaching the fort's landing. In the foreground is Mendota. Painting Minnesota Historical Society.

cross the two sets of rapids. She had to stop often to send out wooding parties and always stopped at sundown. Yet she made the trip to Fort Snelling, at the confluence of the Minnesota and Mississippi rivers, much faster than any other transportation available at the time could have done.

Virginia completed two more trips above the rapids in 1823, once as far as Fort Snelling and another to Fort Crawford at Prairie du Chien, Wisconsin. On her second trip from St. Louis to the Minnesota River, she repassed a keelboat she had already passed once on her first trip upriver. The keelboat was still toiling on its first trip to Galena, Illinois. How much faster this new mode of transport could be!

Following *Virginia,* in September 1823, a new sidewheel packet operating out of Nashville became the second steamboat to cross the rapids and run on the upper river. The 118-ton *Rambler,* under command of Captain Bruce, brought up supplies to Fort Snelling, and when she left she took down two Swiss families who had traveled to the fort overland from Selkirk's Colony (Winnipeg), thus demonstrating the Mississippi River could be an outlet for Canadian goods as well. A new era had dawned in the Upper Mississippi Valley.

Crossing the Lower Rapids in 1835

As we were to be detained here [Fort Edwards, now Warsaw, Illinois] awhile, M. [Charles A. Murray] and myself called upon Colonel Kearney, the commanding officer, and his lady, and were asked to dine. In the meantime, the cargo of the steamer, which consisted principally of pigs of lead, was shifted into flat-bottomed barges, on account of the Des Moines Rapids, which we had now to pass over, and which extended twelve miles below this place, the rocks in many places, coming to within two feet of the surface.

The steamer being lightened, we re-embarked, and after a good many rude bumps on the bottom, got clear of these shallows, and reached a sorry settlement on the left bank, called Keokuk, after a celebrated Sauk chief, inhabited altogether by a set of desperadoes of this part of the Mississippi. . . .

Our steamer had now become a Babel of noise and vulgarity; drinking, smoking, swearing, and gambling prevailed from morn to night; the captain of the steamer refusing to suppress any of these irregularities. . . . At noon we reached St. Louis, and landing found that all the hotels were full, not a room being to be had for love or money. This was not very pleasant to a couple of Englishmen disgusted with the dirt and ribaldry of a western steamer.

G. W. Featherstonhaugh, *A Canoe Voyage Up the Minnay Sotor*

CHAPTER FIVE

Steamboats Open the West and Defend the Frontier

Military officials realized at once that chartered steamboats were the best way to move men and supplies to far-flung frontier posts. In 1824 the *General Neville* supplied Fort Snelling (*Virginia,* her fate typical of early river boats, was out of commission, having hit a snag and sunk the previous fall). She was followed by the *Rufus Putnam* in 1825.

By the end of May 1826 some eighteen boats had made at least one trip to the St. Peters, as the area around Fort Snelling and the mouth of the St. Peters, or Minnesota, River came to be known. Among these, as noted by Indian Agent Taliaferro, were *Mandan, Indiana, Lawrence, Eclipse, Scioto, Josephine, Fulton, Red Rover, Black Rover, Warrior, Enterprise* and *Volant.* That year the *Lawrence* became the first steamboat to ascend the Mississippi River above Fort Snelling, going within three and one-half miles of the Falls of St. Anthony.

All of these boats had been built on the Ohio River, at boatyards in and near Pittsburgh (Pennsylvania), Cincinnati, Gallipolis and Marietta (Ohio), Newport and Louisville (Kentucky), and New Albany and Jeffersonville (Indiana).

Most of them were medium-sized packets of about 100 tons capacity that usually operated from New Orleans to Memphis or St. Louis. For many years the only steamers to run on the upper Mississippi were chartered by the government or by the big Indian trading firms that operated out of St. Louis and Prairie du Chien, Wisconsin.

Moving Troops and Supplies

Steamboats became invaluable to quickly move troops and supplies where they were needed on the frontier. The Mississippi River was the chief avenue of transportation and communication between the upper river outposts. In 1828, *Missouri* was chartered to move eight companies of infantry from Jefferson Barracks, near St. Louis, to outposts on the Upper Mississippi. In 1831 and 1832 Capt. James May's *Enterprise* transported troops from Jefferson Barracks to Rock Island and Prairie du Chien to quell disturbances between incoming settlers and the displaced Sac and Fox (Mesquakie) Indians.

A `Speck of War' on the Mississippi

At the outbreak of the Black Hawk War in Wisconsin in 1832, several steamboats were pressed into government service: *Chieftain* and *Enterprise* were used to shuttle troops from St. Louis to Prairie du Chien. Steamboats plying the river were first to bring news of the war to downriver ports; some, such as *Dove,* were actually fired upon by the Sac Indians.

Captain Joseph Throckmorton was ordered to patrol the upper river with his single-deck sidewheeler *Warrior* to prevent the Indians crossing. A detachment of soldiers was put on board and a small cannon mounted to the bow. *Warrior* steamed north to Wabasha's village (near present Winona), and on her return at the Bad Axe River, near the present village of De Soto, Wisconsin, she engaged Black Hawk's soldiers in a battle. After trading shots for a hour, the steamer broke off for lack of fuel and continued on to Prairie du Chien. *Warrior* remained a government scout and transport until after the close of that war.

Steamboats Eagerly Awaited

A great difficulty on the Upper Mississippi was that the river was frozen at least five months out of the year, bringing all travel and commerce to a halt. The first steamboat of the season to make it through Lake Pepin, usually the last part of the river to lose its ice, was greeted with unconcealed delight by the people living at the St. Peters. *Versailles* was the first boat up in May 1832, bringing with her the first supplies the post had seen since the preceding November.

Through the 1830s arrivals were noted at Fort Snelling of the *Enterprise, Warrior, Palmyra, Saint Peters, Missouri Fulton, Frontier* and several others that were not named by the chronicler, Indian Agent Lawrence Taliaferro.

At the battle of Bad Axe the **Warrior** helped stop the Sac leader Black Hawk at the Mississippi and bring an end to the 1832 war. **Warrior** was commissioned by the army and issued a cannon. Lithograph by Henry Lewis in *Das Illustrirte Mississippithal.*

An early sidewheeler, the **Missouri** was kept busy transporting troops and supplies to frontier posts on the upper Mississippi in the late 1820s and was at Fort Snelling in 1828. Drawing Murphy Library, University of Wisconsin–La Crosse.

Visiting the "Great White Father"

As the United States began to acquire Indian lands, steamboating was stimulated directly by the need to transport delegations of Indians and commissioners to the treaty grounds and by the yearly delivery of annuity goods to the bands that had ceded their lands. Even though the first steamboats puffing up the Mississippi were viewed with alarm by many Indians, those bands living near the river soon became accustomed to the "monsters" and at times vied for the opportunity to take a trip on a steamboat.

More than 300 Sac, Fox, Otoe and Iowa Indians were taken by steamboat to Prairie du Chien in July of 1830, where they and delegates of the Dakota and Winnebago signed a treaty creating a neutral strip in Iowa and Minnesota between the warring tribes. They were returned to their homes on the *Red Rover,* a boat that habitually operated above the Lower Rapids. Over time, the boats became associated with the arrival of their yearly annuities and the arrival of a steamboat at an Indian village always produced a crowd to meet her. Harriet Bishop, St. Paul's first schoolteacher, noted as she arrived at Little Crow's village on the *Lynx* in 1847: "The ringing of the bell occasioned a grand rush, and with telegraphic speed, every man, woman, and child flew to the landing."

In 1837 Governor Henry Dodge of Wisconsin Territory set out for Fort Snelling on *Irene* to negotiate a treaty with the Ojibwe, whereby the first land in what is now Minnesota and a part of northern Wisconsin was ceded to the

United States. That same summer, Agent Lawrence Taliaferro was ordered to bring a delegation of Dakota Indians to Washington to negotiate a treaty. Taliaferro chartered Captain James Lafferty's steamer *Pavilion,* which was boarded at Kaposia by Wakinyantanka (Chief Little Crow) and his pipe bearer. At Red Wing Wakute and other Mdewakanton Dakota came on board, and at the present site of Winona, Chiefs Wabasha and Etuzepah joined the delegation.

Twenty-six Indians made the journey on *Pavilion* down the Mississippi and up the Ohio to Pittsburgh, then journeyed overland to Washington City by a combination of canal, railroad and stagecoach. On September 29 they signed a treaty relinquishing their claims to the St. Croix Valley. The return journey took a month; all made it back safely in November despite a boiler explosion on board their boat, the *Rolla,* below Rock Island.

As soon as the lands in Iowa and east of the Mississippi in what is now in Minnesota and Wisconsin were open to settlement, steamboats began arriving at Fort Snelling with great regularity. *Rolla* and *Pavilion* came in 1837; *Gipsy* also arrived that year and returned in 1838 with annuity goods for the Ojibwe. By June 1838 *Burlington* had made three trips to Fort Snelling to bring 146 recruits and supplies for the Fifth Infantry, and on June 15 the garrison was treated to the novelty of two boats in at same time when *Brazil* puffed up alongside *Burlington.*

Influx of Traders and Settlers

Not all arrivals were logged at Fort Snelling. Steamboats were used from the beginning by the fur companies to supply their Upper Mississippi posts. When Captain David Bates took the *Rufus Putnam* to Fort Snelling in 1825, he also carried goods for the Columbia Fur Company, which

---

1838 Annuities Payment

The crew and passengers of the Palmyra had been greatly annoyed by the Indians, who expected their first payment in July and besieged the boat in great numbers, demanding it at the hands of the first whites who had come up the river . . . . It was not until the first week of November that their goods came for payment. The place where Stillwater now stands was selected as the place where they should assemble.

The old stern wheel Gipsey [sic] brought the goods and landed them on the beach. The Chippewas came there to the number of 1,100 in their canoes, nearly starved by waiting for their payment. While there receiving it the river and lake froze up, and a deep snow came on; thus all their supplies, including one hundred barrels of flour, twenty-five of pork, kegs of tobacco, bales of blankets, guns and ammunition, casks of Mexican dollars, etc., all were sacrificed except what they could carry off on their backs through the snow hundreds of miles away. Their fleet of birch canoes they destroyed before leaving, lest the Sioux might have the satisfaction of doing the same after they left. . . . The old Gypsey had scarcely time to get through the lake before the ice formed.

Levi Stratton, account in W. H. C. Folsom *Fifty Years in the Northwest,* 1888

he off-loaded at their depot at Land's End, about one mile up the Minnesota River, making the *Putnam* the first steamboat known to have ascended that river, if only a short distance.

In 1836 *Bellevue* arrived carrying Indian trade goods and supplies to the American Fur Company depot at Mendota, a small settlement across the Minnesota River from the fort. American Fur Company principals also owned part of the sternwheeler *Ariel,* which in 1838 and 1839 began making regular runs from St. Louis to Grey Cloud Island, Red Rock (Newport) and Mendota with trade goods and provisions. These boats made the return journeys loaded with furs and passengers.

Mills at St. Croix Falls, Wisconsin, begun in 1838 with supplies brought up on the steamboat **Palmyra.** Painting by Henry Lewis c.1850. Minneapolis Institute of Arts.

Fayette brought up stores for the fort's sutler, or storekeeper, in April 1839. *Glaucus* made two trips that year. She was probably the first boat to land at St. Paul's Lower Landing where she off-loaded six barrels of whiskey for trader David Faribault, who was operating a store there for St. Paul's premier settler, the notorious "Pigs Eye" Parrant. At that time Faribault had no neighbors, but by the end of 1839, five French Canadian families and a few single men had begun a settlement on the bluff called Imnijaska or White Rock, now St. Paul. Other boats to arrive in 1839 were *Pennsylvania, Knickerbocker, Malta, Pike* and *Des Moines.*

Collectively, these small settlements near Fort Snelling and the mouth of the Minnesota River (then called the St. Peters River) were known as "the St. Peters," and most steamers were noted as "loading for the St. Peters." As sawmills and villages began to develop on the St. Croix River, some of these boats also started making trips up that river.

Early Traffic on the St. Croix

No steamboats had reason to venture into the St. Croix Valley until the summer of 1838, when the lands on both sides of the river became open to settlement. Steamboat traffic on that river commenced when lumbermen from eastern states began to scout out likely sawmill sites. The first steamer known to have dipped its paddlewheels in St. Croix waters was the old sidewheeler *Palmyra* that had left St. Louis July 5, 1838, heavily laden. Aboard her were fifty workmen plus millwright Calvin Tuttle, along with provisions for four months and equipment to build the first sawmill in the St. Croix Valley. Captain William Middleton stopped first at Fort Snelling on July 15 to bring notice that Congress had approved the Indian treaties of 1837, which made the lands east of the Mississippi River available for enterprise and settlement. He then nosed *Palmyra* past the bar at Point Douglas and proceeded upriver, reaching the falls of the St. Croix on July 17, 1838. Work began on the sawmill immediately.

Three months later, on September 29, Captain Joseph Throckmorton's *Ariel* plowed up the river as far as the site of Stillwater, where she landed an exploring party from a lumbering firm formed the previous winter at Marine Settlement, Illinois. David Hone and Lewis Judd had been sent to scout the river to find the best site for a sawmill, but the water was too low for the steamer, so they poled a flatboat the rest of the way, eventually locating a claim at what is now Marine on St. Croix.

The third boat to enter the river in 1838 was *Gipsy,* carrying the long-overdue Ojibwe annuity goods. After grounding once in Lake St. Croix, which is the lower part of the St. Croix River, she landed the Indians' money, tools and provisions at the head of the lake and left hurriedly, just ahead of an early winter. (For the rest of the story, see the box on page 35.)

In mid-May 1839 the sidewheeler *Fayette*,

Marine Mills, settled 1839, became a thriving lumber town. This c.1880 woodcut by Peter Hugunine shows the popular St. Croix-built sternwheeler, **G. B. Knapp**. Print Washington County Historical Society.

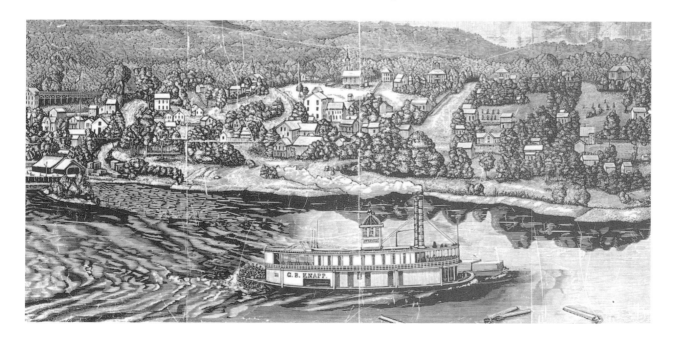

appeared on the St. Croix. On her were eight partners of the Marine Mills Company, the millwright, blacksmith and Mrs. David Hone, who was to be the company cook. *Fayette* also had a heavy cargo consisting of the machinery for the mill to be built at Marine, along with provisions, farming tools, household goods and livestock to sustain the settlement. That July another Throckmorton boat, *Malta,* arrived at Fort Snelling with annuity goods for the Dakota. She had many dignitaries on board, and on the twenty-fourth she made the first excursion trip on Lake St. Croix (the lower part of the St. Croix River), taking her passengers to see the battleground, now in downtown Stillwater, where the Dakota and Ojibwe had had a fight earlier that summer,

The following year several boats chugged up the St. Croix River, most freighting mill supplies, annuity goods and loggers and some carrying curious tourists. Noted on the lake in 1840 were *Annie, Indian Queen, General Pike* and *Brazil.* Eighty colonists looking for site to build their new community chartered a boat called

the *Eldora* in St. Louis that year. They are supposed to have entered the St. Croix and reached Joseph R. Brown's warehouse at the head of the lake, now the Dutchtown section of Stillwater, but what happened to the colonists or the boat is not recorded.

In April 1841 the *Tennessee* arrived at St. Croix Falls. She had on board equipment and supplies for the sawmill, as well as the mill owners, who had spent the winter in St. Louis. Also arriving in 1841 were *Otter, Chippewa, Sarah Ann* and *Rock River,* the first three owned by the American Fur Company.

Up to this time, all the boats arriving at Fort Snelling or on the St. Croix were charters carrying excursion passengers or supplies for the fort, trading houses and mills. No captain would make the long journey north without assurance of adequate cargo to pay for the trip. As settlements were formed, an occasional itinerant boat chugged up the river hoping to do some business, or just out of curiosity, but not until 1842 could residents count on regular steamboat service north of Galena.

CHAPTER SIX

The St. Peters Becomes a Destination

As soon as there were steamboat capable ascending the Upper Mississippi, were tourists on them. The first tourist to arrive by steamboat at the St. Peters—the virtual head of navigation on the Mississippi—was a colorful Italian adventurer named Giacomo Beltrami, who took passage in April 1823 on the maiden voyage of *Virginia*.

Beltrami was not the only passenger on this first steamboat to travel on the Upper Mississippi, and although the other travelers had business at Galena and Prairie du Chien, all were eager to spend a few hours gawking at the tourist sights. Beltrami played the consummate tourist by keeping a chronicle of the journey, complete with exhaustive descriptions of the upper river, which reminded him of the Rhine.

In the early years of steamboating, a large proportion of the visitors was connected with the army or other government agencies. Still, many of them acted like tourists, writing back home about the breathtaking sights to be seen. Every government exploring party had with it a naturalist who made note of the exotic flora and fauna to be found there and whose reports excited people's interest in the "far west" when they were published.

Fort Snelling was the only outpost of American civilization north of Prairie du Chien, and for years almost all tourists were dependent upon the fort's hospitality.

John Bliss, son of Fort Snelling's commander, recalled that in 1832, while en route to his father's post on the *Warrior,* he saw no house

Excursionists on the Mississippi River thrilled to the "romantic solitude" of the scenery, especially at Lake Pepin where the precipitous bluffs reminded them of turreted castles. View along the Mississippi near Maiden Rock. Watercolor by Edwin Whitefield, c. 1856. Minnesota Historical Society.

or white person north of Prairie du Chien. He commented on the many visitors who were hospitably received at the fort, entertained with picnics on the prairie, and given escorted tours to Little Falls (Minnehaha), St. Anthony's Falls, the Indian village at Lake Calhoun and Fountain Cave (on the Mississippi just west of St. Paul). Many were also treated to a display of dancing or a game of lacrosse performed by the Dakota bands that lived near the fort. By 1835 the number of seasonal visitors at the Fort was said to be between one and two hundred.

Tourists Flock to "See the Elephant"

Western sightseers were driven by a passion to see nature in her unspoiled simplicity and beauty. Many people condemned the technological advances and social changes made during the industrial revolution as having eroded traditional American virtues, but these virtues were thought to be still alive in the west.

Jaded easterners, steeped in the literature, poetry and art of the romantic movement, sought the utopia of the American frontier. They came for the picturesque scenery, to observe the Indians (deemed to be "children of nature") and to take part in writing sentimental journals about their travels. In the parlance of the day, they flocked "to see the elephant"—an expression reserved for the biggest, most wonderful, most popular sight.

Their view of the west was largely shaped by other travelers' florid accounts, and, after 1839, by enormously popular traveling panoramas.

Picnickers at Minnehaha Falls, a favorite resort of excursionists to Fort Snelling who were often driven to the site in carriages from the fort. Photo B. F. Upton c.1868, Minnesota Historical Society.

These were twelve-foot-wide canvases painted to depict the scenery along the river, which were unrolled before the viewer to recreate a trip on the great river. Panoramas did much to popularize the Mississippi as a tourist destination. But newspapers, especially those published in western cities, were the leading promoters of western travel. And the Mississippi steamboat was the means that made it possible for adventurous tourists to indulge their love of nature while traveling comfortably ensconced in a floating hotel, attracted by, as one said, a "curious blending of savage and civilized life."

The Fashionable Tour

While some travelers were people connected with the military taking their families on a tour of frontier posts, others were pure tourists, intent on visiting Fort Snelling and viewing that "Niagara of the West," the Falls of St. Anthony. Among them, in the spring of 1835, were George Catlin and his wife with one of several "pleasure parties" brought up by Captain Joseph Throckmorton's *Warrior*. It was Catlin who gave the "fashionable tour" its name.

Catlin, who had come west to sketch and paint the Indians, was enthralled with the "wild and native grandeur and majesty of this great Western world." Enthusing upon the "magnificence of the scenes which are continually opening to the eye of the traveller, and riveting him to the deck of the steamer, through sunshine, lightning or rain, from the mouth of the Ouisconsin [Wisconsin] to the Fall of St. Anthony," he finished by suggesting that tourists make their next "Fashionable Tour" on the Upper Mississippi. Catlin's glowing reports spurred tourism on

the Mississippi. The following year travelers flocked to the St. Peters area. They came from the eastern and southern United States as well as from England, France, Russia and other countries.

Among the steamboats carrying excursionists in 1836 were Captain G. B. Cole's *Palmyra* and Captain Throckmorton's new boat, cleverly named for her destination, *Saint Peters*. Elizabeth Schuyler Hamilton, widow of Alexander Hamilton, added her stamp of approval after a delightful voyage to the fort in 1837 on *Burlington*, along with hundreds more happy tourists who arrived on *Missouri Fulton*, *Rolla* and *Irene*. While trip destinations sometimes depended on the cargoes offered, excursionists often outnumbered other passengers on these packets.

A fresh-water stream issued forth from Fountain Cave, a popular tourist spot halfway between St. Paul and Fort Snelling and reachable by steamboat. By 1852 a pavilion and footbridge had been installed for the comfort of visitors. Anonymous sketch c. 1850. Minnesota Historical Society.

Galena Merchants Promote Mississippi Tourism

The five Harris brothers and A. G. Montford of Galena were among the earliest promoters of steamboat tourism. By 1837, Smith Harris was advertising an excursion to the Falls of Saint Anthony in *Smelter,* a new sidewheeler and one of the first boats to boast private staterooms, "should a sufficient number of passengers present themselves."

The Harrises believed that tourists would patronize those boats offering the best facilities, and so *Smelter* was offered up as the fastest, most luxurious and largest craft on the Upper Mississippi. Two years later the Harris brothers brought out *Pizarro,* a "commodious" boat that boasted a fire pump and hose attached to her engine "for immediate use in case of fire." Tourist excursions became an annual event for the Galena merchants. In June 1845 Smith Harris was offering to the citizens of Dubuque a two-week excursion to the Falls of Saint Anthony in the first *War Eagle,* described as a "new and splendid" boat. His advertisement promised that it would be "a pleasure excursion in *reality,* and will stop at all places of amusement as long as the passengers may desire."

That same year, in June of 1845, *Time & Tide,* commanded by Smith Harris, and *Lightfoot,* captained by A. G. Montford, set off from Galena for Fort Snelling with a crowd of merrymakers. They left with the bows of the boats lashed together—*Time* serving as promenade and dance salon, *Lightfoot* as dining hall and hotel. The passengers were free to pass from boat to boat and, while the boats were "wooding up" as they had to do every thirty miles or so, were also free to prowl about scenic and historic spots on shore. Lafayette Bunnell was on that trip and left the fascinating account on the next page.

Where to Go on Vacation?

The 1840s were truly the heyday of tourism on the upper river. As the number of travelers grew, captains were able to give their entire boats over to excursions. Dozens of boats advertised large and fashionable pleasure parties "to the Indian country and Falls of St. Anthony" commencing in settlements as widely separated as Pittsburgh, New Orleans and St. Louis. As these voyages were quite profitable, upper river captains began to offer several excursions each season, often taking along representatives of the newspapers who obligingly wrote glowing testimonials. Gushed a Galena editor, such a "summer jaunt" answered the onerous question of "those harassed as to where to go on a vacation

PLEASURE EXCURSION.
FOR ST. PETERS & FALLS OF ST. ANTHONY

The splendid, safe and commodious passenger steamboat MONSOON, C. G. Pearce, master, will leave Louisville the 6th June, for a trip of pleasure. Those who wish to enjoy this delightful excursion, may be assured that no efforts of the captain will be wanting to make them happy.
C. BASHAM, Jr., Agent,
No. 11. Com. Row.
may 26

This advertisement for the "fashionable tour" appeared in the *Louisville Journal,* June 4, 1840. Originally published in *Minnesota History 20,* Dec. 1939.

Excursion to Fort Snelling, 1845.

Upon entering Lake Pepin the steamboats were separated, and for the amusement of the tourists, a race was projected to Red Wing. At the very commencement, the writer was informed by Keeler Harris, the engineer, that the race would be a slow one, as Captain Smith Harris . . . had ordered the slowest boat to win. Therefore, said Keeler, who was my especial friend, don't you lose any money on this race, nor do you give me away, for it will be a very close race.

Keeler Harris' prediction proved true, for one boat would seem to be at the point of passing the other, when a little sperm oil or a side of fat bacon thrown into the furnace would put new life into the lagging craft, and, as though it were a thing of life, it would seem encouraged by the lusty huz-zahs of its passengers, and shoot ahead again of its snorting antagonist. In that way, to the great enjoyment of the passengers on the winning boat, and the chagrin of those on the beaten one, we ran to Red Wing. . . . On the return passage through the lake, an opportunity was given the losers to recover their losses, but their lack of fidelity to their first favorite caused many to change their bets, and as the winner was the other boat in the second race, the losers declared that there had been as much jockeying as in a horse race, and Keeler Harris and the writer believed them.

On the arrival of the boats at Fort Snelling, the officers and their wives and daughters, received the tourists with cordiality, and with what conveyances could be improvised by the quartermaster, and with a few carriages taken up for the purpose on the boats, we drove to Minnehaha and St. Anthony Falls, while a few rode horses, and enjoyed a grand pic-nic, cooling the potations of various kinds in springs and in the spray of the falls. At early twilight we returned to the boats, and found that arrangements had been made for entertaining those from the fort inclined to dance. . . .

As the night waned, the dance closed, and with cheerful farewells to our guests of the fort, we slowly steamed down to a landing near to the present Union depot of St. Paul. . . . We were compelled to tie up to await the passing of very dark clouds that threatened our safe passage of the "hog's back" bend in the river; and while so waiting, a few of us, for continued diversion, climbed the steep hill to the only house of prominence, Jackson's, except a small chapel on the plateau that is now occupied by St. Paul. . . .

In the twilight of early dawn, and with a cargo of valuable furs, we once more started down the river, this time in single file until we should reach the head of Lake Pepin. . . . We were once more united at Cratte's, now Wabasha, where taking on more furs and some passengers from the Chippewa valley, we steamed on below, stopping at Holmes' Landing and Wapasha prairie (Winona), where we stayed for some time for the amusement and entertainment of the passengers while they bartered for curios among the Indians, who were, many of them, encamped above the landing at the foot of Center street, on the higher ground; and then, after a quick run and a short stop at La Crosse, the excursionists were once more carried back to civilization and their homes.

Lafayette H. Bunnell, *Winona and Its Environs on the Mississippi in Ancient and Modern Days,* 1897

VIEW OF ST ANTHONY, MINNEAPOLIS AND ST ANTHONY'S FALLS.

The earliest excursion to the Falls of St. Anthony (now Minneapolis) was made by the steamboat **Lawrence** in 1826. Even after the waterpower began to be developed and the river bridged, as in this 1857 view, the falls were still a popular tourist attraction, and there was an active landing at the village of St. Anthony. Lithograph by Edwin Whitefield, Minnesota Historical Society.

At a cost of only $4 or $5 (the equivalent of about $100 today), they could enjoy an inexpensive five- or six-day outing on an Upper Mississippi steamboat. And the best part for many excursion passengers was that they often did not have to share the boat with freight, livestock and deck passengers, making a much more pleasant voyage.

By the mid-1840s increasing competition had forced steamboat owners to offer more conveniences, novelties and amenities to their guests to go along with the romantic scenery.

Boats advertised private staterooms with their own wash-stands, comfortable beds with spring mattresses, music provided by a well-known band or orchestra, the finest comestibles, evening entertainments such as lectures and dances and jaunts to the leading tourist attractions. Passengers might also arrange for fishing parties or camping out under the stars.

Tour boats were often decked out with fresh evergreens and flower garlands, and some carried rockets or fireworks to amuse the passengers and announce their presence. Some got so festive-looking they seemed, as one viewer put it, to be a floating shrubbery.

Fourth of July excursions became very popular, many promising substantial meals and an orchestra to furnish music for dancing. Other boats promoted romantic cruises, as newspaper advertisements exhorted readers to "Gather up your sweethearts" for an excursion "by the light of the silvery moon." Captains reaped rich profits as local civic and fraternal groups chartered their boats for one- or two-day trips.

Competition for the tourist dollar became fierce. In a three-week period in 1845 the public was given a choice of four excursions from

---

A Moonlight Cruise in 1853

One of these pleasant and social reunions which our packet captains are such adepts at getting up -- none more so than Capt. M. W. Lodwick of the stately Ben Campbell-- came off on board this favorite steamer on Saturday evening last.... [A]bout dusk the boat pushed out from our landing carrying afloat a goodly number of our citizens.... The excursion was a moonlight trip to Ft. Snelling and back, the occasion embraced by Capt. Lodwick to provide a most sumptuous entertainment in the regal salons of his river home.

Weekly Minnesotian, (St. Paul), May 8, 1853

Galena to the St. Peters—Captain John Atchison with the *Lynx,* Captain Hiram Bersie with the *Saint Croix,* Captain D. B. Morehouse with *Iowa* and Smith Harris with *War Eagle.* In 1853 the *Die Vernon, New Saint Paul* and the *Dr. Franklin* all arrived at once at the St. Paul levee with excursion parties. On that occasion, as he often did,

Captain Preston Lodwick threw a party on board the *Franklin*, inviting the leading citizens of St. Paul to join in.

Steamboat excursions remained popular through the 1850s, although Fort Snelling was no longer the destination, having been overtaken by the burgeoning St. Paul, which was incorporated as a city in 1854. The success of the Great Excursion in June of that year encouraged a host of imitators who promised to provide passengers with every conceivable amusement "no pains spared." With the advent of regular passenger service, many tourists also traveled on the regular packets. "The boats continue to come loaded with passengers, many of them seeking only recreation," said St. Paul's *Minnesota Pioneer* in 1852. "Boats are crowded down and up. Some travel for the sake of economy and save the expense of tavern bills at home."

One of those travelers in the summer of 1852 was New Yorker Elizabeth Ellet, a writer of history and travel books. She took passage on the big, new *Ben Campbell,* pride of the Galena, Dubuque and Minnesota Packet Company. So taken was she with this mode of travel, she refused to give up her seat on the guards when asked to sit in the ladies' cabin, which had been elegantly furnished with velvet draperies, easy chairs and carpeting.

After taking the "grand tour" from St. Paul, Mrs. Ellet boarded the smaller *Black Hawk* for a cruise up the St. Croix River with Captain and Mrs. W. P. Hall. Although a light-draft boat, the heavily laden *Black Hawk* grounded several times on sandbars, testing even Mrs. Ellet's patience, but at last made it through to St. Croix Falls. Still thrilled with all she saw, this indomitable travel writer returned to Galena on Orrin Smith's *Nominee,* which she later wrote up as "the finest boat on the upper Mississippi."

On to St. Anthony's Falls, and Other Wonders

Although most boats advertised their excursion would go to the Falls of St. Anthony, few of them actually went so far. During the summer months, the high season for travel, low water and the fast current generally prevented boats from reaching the head of navigation.

Passengers were discharged at Fort Snelling, and driven the last eight miles to the cataract in carriages. In 1826 the *Lawrence* ventured to within three and one-half miles of the falls, but dared not go farther. No boats made it until 1850, a high-water year, when a purse of $250 (worth well over $5,000 today) was offered for the first boat to reach the Falls of St. Anthony. *Lamartine,* commanded by Captain J. W. Marsh,

Elizabeth Ellet's boat **Ben Campbell**, shown here gaily decorated with evergreens near Buffalo, Iowa, c. 1855, was in its day the biggest, most luxurious boat on the upper river boasting fifty large staterooms and a grand salon. But the 287-ton steamer was a bit large for the St. Paul run and was sold in 1853 after grounding on Pig's Eye bar in sight of St. Paul. Photo Minnesota Historical Society.

came within a mile of the cataract, but Captain Dan Able collected the prize in the *Anthony Wayne*, ascending to the village of St. Anthony, which straddled the falls on the east bank. "In the evening," reported the *Minnesota Pioneer*, "there was a ball in the cabin of the boat and a glorious good time." That same summer Captain Able took an excursion party up the Minnesota River as far as what is today Carver, making the *Wayne* the first steamboat to ascend that river any distance. Both boats also were on the St. Croix River that season, and *Lamartine* managed to claw her way some distance up the Apple River, a small tributary of the St. Croix.

Navigation of Upper Mississippi tributaries began in the 1830s, but boats that plied the Wisconsin, Potosi, Black, Chippewa, Des Moines, Iowa and Turkey rivers carried few tourists. Early excursionists were primarily attracted to the St. Croix and Minnesota rivers.

Probably the first sightseeing trip on the St. Croix was that made in 1839 by Joseph Throckmorton's *Malta* to cater to the morbid curiosity of his passengers who wished to view an Indian battleground (Battle Hollow, now in Stillwater). The St. Croix is well described as "a stream of surpassing beauty, a kaleidoscopic panorama, bringing delightful scenery to view with every turn of the stream," and of course it appealed to the romantic tourist. After a few years most excursion boats that went to the St. Peters also took a turn on the St. Croix River.

Captain George B. Cole was the first to attempt the Minnesota River in 1836 when he ascended about three miles with an excursion party on *Palmyra*. In the high-water year of 1850 several adventuresome excursion parties attempted the Minnesota River, making a contest of which could get the furthest. Captain Dan Able took the 164-ton sidewheeler *Anthony Wayne* up as far as the Little Rapids, just upriver of present Carver, Minnesota. Not to be outdone, Orrin Smith steamed up in July, passed the rapids and planted the *Nominee's* shingle three miles above. The *Wayne* tried again, getting as far as Traverse des Sioux (now St. Peter), only to be bested by the Harrises' sternwheeler *Yankee*, which reached a point well above the site of Mankato a week later. It was reported that Captain Keeler Harris wanted to go farther, but the passengers complained that it was too hot, there were swarms of mosquitoes and, besides (and most important), the provisions were running low, so the boat was turned back.

A shallow river with a short boating season and a difficult rapids that often required a portage and a change of boats, the Minnesota River was never as appealing to excursionists as the St. Croix, but became instead a busy artery filled with townsite developers and immigrants.

CHAPTER SEVEN

Packet Companies and Pirate Craft

*B*ecause of its northern geography and its stunning topography, the northern part of the Mississippi remained a river of wilderness scenery, romance and adventure, attracting tourists, but devoid of commercial interest.

For the first two decades of the steamboat era—the 1820s and '30s—most of the traffic consisted of lower Mississippi and Ohio River boats that had been chartered to deliver military forces and government supplies. Some early steamers were owned or hired by the fur companies to carry goods to their far-flung trading posts and return with the fur harvest. As the land opened for settlement, eastern businessmen who saw the lumbering potential also hired boats to haul up their mill equipment, laborers and supplies. Most travelers had to make a bargain with one of these chartered boats to book passage to the St. Peters area. Independent steamboat captains would not make the trip unless they had guaranteed freight.

Generally an Ohio River boat, the **Ben West** sometimes ran charters or prospected for business as a "wild boat" on the upper Mississippi. Lithograph c.1849, Murphy Library, University of Wisconsin–La Crosse.

Transients, or Wild Boats

Until the 1850s transient steamers, often called "wild boats," were the most numerous on the upper river. These independent boats were freelance carriers, usually captained by their owner, who took them river to river and port to port looking for business. Needing no docks or freight houses, they would stop at any sandbank for cargo or passengers. Many centered their operations at larger river ports, where they could simply hang out their shingle advertising a destination and date of departure.

Transients were important to the developing river trade because they could easily adjust to the seasonal and regional flow of business. Where there was a lot of business, more boats appeared, and as they offered highly competitive rates, shipping expenses remained low.

On the other hand, the wild boats lacked punctuality, regularity and reliability. No one could anticipate when a captain might see his way clear to making a paying trip; he might linger at a larger port, hoping to pick up more business, or cut his voyage short if he felt it would not pay expenses. The captain of a transient steamboat felt no compunction to arrive at his destination at a given time. He was usually more interested in picking up additional business along the river. If the anticipated business failed to materialize, he might abandon the trip altogether and turn his cargo over to some other boat.

There were instances of passengers and their luggage being marooned on a sandbar when the captain of the tramp determined that the freight and passengers were no longer profitable. Sometimes the passengers on the boat managed

Why a Captain Might Fib a Bit

The fact was, that our captain had advertised to go to Louisville at a very low fare, and had by that means succeeded in getting passengers, who, tempted by the prospect of saving money, neglected the opportunity of going on board one of the regular Louisville boats. It was not for me to reproach him; I was a voluntary passenger, and it was my interest to be upon good terms with him. I therefore, in a good-humoured tone, asked him if his going to Louisville was really a joke; upon which he frankly told me, that the advertisement he had put out at St. Louis was only a decoy, adding: "Why, doctor, you must see, that if I had advertised for such a place as this, I shouldn't have got not a beginning of a passenger in a month."

. . .About noon we saw a steamer bearing down on us. . . ."Then," said I, "you always set this trap for people, and they know it, I suppose in yon steamer?" "Why, doctor," replied he, "I know it ain't right; but you can't get on no how on this river without lying a little."

George W. Featherstonhaugh, *A Canoe Voyage Up the Minnay Sotor,* 2, 1847

to prevail on their captain by bribes to obtain through passage to their destination. But it more often occurred, as a traveler in 1828 recorded, "If the captain determines that his freight and passengers will not pay expenses or yield profit, he will `go no further' —he will refund as much as he pleases and the passenger must make a new bargain if he can . . . He will detain as long as there is a box or a board or a passenger to get on board."

Low water, bad weather and encroaching ice might also cause a transient to decamp for better climes, although some captains would risk their boats in order to get at the first or last freight of the season, which always commanded a premium price. Sometimes boats of lighter draft would prowl the river during low water to pick up passengers and freight left behind by the larger boats that could go no further. This would be a bonanza for them, as they could charge exorbitant fees.

The Transition to Packet Service

Going A-pirating

When the water in the rivers is low, the large steam vessels very often run aground, and are obliged to discharge their cargoes and passengers. At these times, the smaller steamboats ply up and down the rivers to take advantage of these misfortunes by picking up passengers and making most exorbitant charges for taking them or the goods out, because you *must* pay them or remain where you are. This species of cruising they themselves designate as "going a-pirating."

Frederick Marryat, *A Diary in America*, 1839

The owners of the American Fur Company, which had main depots at Prairie du Chien and Mendota, knew the owners of transient steamboats had them over a barrel; most captains would raise their rates substantially to haul a partial load or to make a run in the face of the fall freeze-up. Even in the mid-1840s only about forty-four boats would reach the St. Peters each year; in the 1830s the average was likely closer to twenty-five. Since the Indian trade business was dependent upon these steamboats for timely deliveries, the Fur Company encouraged those captains who would provide the most regular service. The company owners also purchased financial interests in several boats such as *Burlington, Ariel, Lynx* and *Nominee*.

Cooperative Ventures

One of the best known of the independent river captains was Joseph Throckmorton. He began operating in 1828 from St. Louis with the little 50-ton *Red Rover*, which thrived on the upper Mississippi as a low-water boat. In 1830 Captain Throckmorton, in an effort to gain the confidence of passengers and shippers and eager to have a reliable and profitable business, formed a cooperative association with Captain S. Shallcross of the *Chieftain*. The two boats provided a through service from St. Louis to Galena with *Chieftain* operating regularly between St. Louis and the lower rapids and *Red Rover* plying above. The partners also provided keelboats to transport freight over the rapids in extreme low water.

The association was an immediate success. River business tended to favor the boat that could guarantee goods and passengers would get through to their destination. The next year Captain Throckmorton formed a similar combination with his new boat, *Winnebago,* and Captain James May of the *Enterprise.*

Captain Throckmorton's reputation for reliability brought him a great deal of business from both the government and the American Fur Company, on the Missouri River as well as the Mississippi. Over some forty years in steamboating he owned, in combination with Galena merchants and Fur Company principals, about a dozen steamboats, among them *Saint Peters, Ariel, Burlington, Chippewa, General Brooke* and *Nimrod.* Merchants also liked these cooperative agreements with boat captains. They knew that a partner who shared in the profit or loss would do everything he could to get the goods to their destination safely.

Regular Packet Service Begins on the Upper River

The first regular packet (that is, a boat running a regular route) to operate above Galena appeared in 1841. The *Rock River,* a little 49-ton sidewheeler owned and run by Hungarian-born Agoston Haraszthy, provided regular service on the Wisconsin River as well as on the Upper Mississippi and made a few trips on the Rock

and Des Moines rivers.

From 1841 through 1844 *Rock River* made several trips a year to the Minnesota and St. Croix rivers prospecting for business. For part of the time she was the only unchartered paddlewheel boat on the upper river. It was the *Rock River* that in 1841 ferried boards from mills on the St. Croix to St. Paul's Landing to finish the little log Chapel of St. Paul, which was the bare beginnings of the city of St. Paul.

However, the *Rock River* lacked power and speed and in 1844, unable to escape the freeze-up of Lake Pepin, was caught in the ice near Wacouta, at the head of the lake. The cook and other employees had to walk out on the ice to La Crosse. The following spring Captain Haraszthy sold the boat to the New Orleans trade to operate on the bayous where she was better able cope with the currents.

Flat-bottomed riverboats could run up on a sandbar to load and unload passengers and cargo. Slowly turning paddlewheels held them there and then reversed to let them back off. Transient boats made the most of this ability and could respond to a hail from shore. Photo Murphy Library, University of Wisconsin–La Crosse.

Two popular Minnesota packets, **Highland Mary** and **Dr. Franklin**, both began their careers on the Ohio River before moving to the Upper Mississippi. They are shown here at the Cincinnati waterfront in 1848. Daguerreotype by Charles Fontayne and William S. Porter, Public Library of Cincinnati and Hamilton County.

The Harris brothers, Galena merchants who were prospering in the lead mining and shipping business, also saw the opportunity offered by the upriver trade. In 1840 they had the sidewheeler *Otter* built at Cincinnati, designing her specifically to compete with American Fur Company boats. *Otter* was commanded by Daniel Smith Harris and his brother Robert Scribe Harris, with James Meeker Harris as engineer and Jackson Harris as bartender and cub pilot. (Fifth brother Martin Keeler Harris also became an engineer and captain.) They ran *Otter* Galena to St. Paul in competition with *Rock River* during the 1842 season and kept her busy in the upper river trade through 1847. Her small size and light draft enabled *Otter* to run in all seasons, and as she towed as many as nine keelboats, she could spread the load and "run on a dew."

Otter broke a shaft at the end of the 1844 season and was laid up at Galena, but the inducements for her to make one more trip were so great that she was run up with but one wheel and barely escaped the ice that closed the river on her return. Her profits persuaded the Harrises to bring out other boats.

The success of the *Otter* also excited the competitive spirit of other captains and more boats came into the upper river trade. In 1843 the sidewheeler *Jasper* kept up with *Otter,* both boats making seven trips to the St. Peters. The following spring several agents of the Fur Company and Captain W. H. Hooper purchased the steamer *Lynx* to assure regular weekly service to the company's depot at Mendota and points in between.

Lynx was unfortunately run aground near

the site of Winona in her first season. She was refloated and taken around to the Ohio where fifteen feet was added to her length, but on her return to the upper river trade she again disappointed her owners by proving to be a most expensive boat to run.

Semi-regular service between Galena and St. Paul began in 1846 when Captain M. W. Lodwick began advertising his little 41-ton sternwheeler, *Argo,* as a regular weekly packet. The Galena to St. Paul run was ideal for a one-week turnaround, as most steamboats could make the trip in about three days up and two to three down. The low-water *Argo* usually towed a barge, which gave her an astonishing cargo capacity for such a small boat—for example, in 1847 she chugged into Galena from St. Croix Falls carrying 100 passengers plus freight.

Argo was sunk in the fall of 1847, but owners Kennedy and M. W. Lodwick soon replaced her, with the intention of continuing weekly packet service. By then other independents were also making weekly or biweekly runs, among them Nick Wall's *Prairie Bird,* E. H. Gleim's *Monona,* and Hiram Bersie's *Saint Croix.*

The Galena & Minnesota Packet Company

The Galena and Minnesota Packet Company (often just Minnesota Packet Company) was organized by M. W. Lodwick and a group of Galena merchants (among them Orrin Smith and Russell Blakeley) over the winter of 1847-48 with the aim of providing regular weekly service to St. Paul and other northern ports. The first boat in the line was the memorable 145-ton packet *Dr. Franklin,* purchased in early 1848 in Cincinnati by captain M. W. Lodwick and Russell Blakeley. Minnesotans Henry H. Sibley and Henry Rice also acquired shares in her. This boat, affec-

Packet Company Organized

I went in with the Galena & St. Paul Packet company. This was a pool, or trust arrangement. The owners put in their boats at an agreed valuation, receiving in evidence stock at $100 a share. All returns and reports were made to the officers of the company, and returns were received in the form of dividends. It was 1854 that this company was organized. Its fleet comprised the Ben Campbell, the Dr. Franklin, the Nominee, the Galena, the War Eagle, and the Alhambra, and its territory lay between Galena and St. Paul.

Capt. W. H. Gabbert, *The Half-Century Democrat* (Davenport), Oct. 22, 1905

tionately known as "The Old Doctor," became a reliable regular at Stillwater and St. Paul through 1853. A few wild boats also fought for a share of the trade; in 1848 John Atchison's *Highland Mary,* Dan Able's *Anthony Wayne* and, during periods of high water, W. H. Hooper's 212-ton *Alexander Hamilton* were among the sixty-three arrivals at St. Paul.

The admission of Wisconsin as a state in 1848 and the creation of Minnesota Territory in 1849 focused everybody's attention on the upper river ports. Icebound St. Paul, practical head of navigation on the river, was the goal, and in ensuing years the mad dash of steamboats for St.

Paul every spring made newspaper headlines up and down the river. Captains vied with each other for the honor of bringing the first boat through Lake Pepin. In truth it was more than an honor, because the first boat often got the lion's share of cargo and was given free wharfage at St. Paul for the rest of the season, a not-in-considerable economic advantage.

First Boats

Before St. Paul had railroad communication with the east, the first steamboat arrival in the spring was an event of much greater importance than now. There was quite a celebration, ending with a dance on the boat—and the steamer was given the freedom of the city, that is, was allowed to use the levee free of wharfage all the season.

The Gate City Weekly (Keokuk) April 30, 1873, quoted in W. J. Peterson, *Steamboats on the Upper Mississippi*, 1937

Rival Companies Enter the Saint Paul Trade

Eager to cash in on the profits to be made in the St. Paul trade, Smith Harris of Galena began a cutthroat competition in 1848 that pitted his fast new packet *Senator* against the *Dr. Franklin.* After considerable rivalry that included reckless racing and a rate war, the Packet Company arranged to buy the *Senator* and put her in their line.

The agreement appears to have been that the Harrises would retire from the Minnesota trade and concentrate on the Galena to St. Louis route. However, the creation of Minnesota Territory promised to bring a big increase in upper river traffic, and this apparently proved too much for the retiring party. In April 1849 the first boat into St. Paul was Smith Harris's big new sidewheeler, quite deliberately named *Dr. Franklin No. 2.* That fall his brother, Captain Keeler Harris, also began running the sternwheeler *Yankee* between St. Paul, Stillwater and Galena.

The struggle between the Harrises and the Minnesota Packet Company went on for three bitter years to the benefit of passengers and freight forwarders, if not of the participating companies. Merchants and settlers took sides, and rates were reduced to a ridiculous figure until a passenger from Galena to St. Paul often paid only fifty cents. During that time the Packet Company had grown to offer three boats a season from Galena. Each captain in the line had to agree to run his boat on a published schedule, departing from Galena or St. Paul at a definite hour on a specific day. In return for keeping to schedule rather than trying to beat out other boats for cargo and passengers, he received a percentage of the profits of the line. The company was also trying to develop a regular line on the Wisconsin River to compete with the light-draft *Newton Waggoner,* an independent doing well running as a regular packet between Galena and Portage.

By 1850 seven regular packets were plying the upper Mississippi and, with the transients, accounting for 104 arrivals at St. Paul. For the 1851 season Dubuque merchants, eager to have their own boat in the profits race, chartered the Wisconsin River steamer *Tiger.* They planned to make two trips a week to St. Paul, but *Tiger's* first trip took six days and she never beat that time (however, *Tiger* later proved her worth on the Minnesota River).

New Saint Paul and **Nominee** at Galena c.1853. **Nominee** ran in the Galena-St. Paul trade for years. Her rival was built by the Harrises for the Galena-St. Paul trade as **Saint Paul**. She proved too slow and too deep and they sold her to Captain James Bissell. At some point she was lengthened and her paddleboxes were relettered **New Saint Paul**. Photo Minnesota Historical Society.

In high water Rufus Ford's *Die Vernon*, the crack boat of the St. Louis and Keokuk Packet line, a 445-ton "floating palace" with over 100 berths, made several trips from St. Louis. Fewer than a third of the 119 boats that came through to St. Paul in 1851 were from St. Louis; most originated in Galena and Dubuque.

In 1852, even before official ratification of treaties with the Dakota Indians that ceded most of southern Minnesota to the United States, immigrants began pouring into the territory. The Packet Company rose to the challenge by acquiring Orrin Smith's *Nominee,* a slick sidewheeler fast enough to make two trips a week from Galena to St. Paul. They also offered the travel-ing public Captain M. W. Lodwick's new first-class packet, *Ben Campbell,* and the *Dr. Franklin* with Russell Blakeley as master. When the *Ben* proved to be too deep and too slow, she was sold and the low-water sidewheeler *Black Hawk* took her place in the line.

Not to be outdone, the Harrises and several other merchants of Galena formed a new com-pany to run a line of first class steamboats

Harris Gave an Interesting Boat Ride

Captain [Smith] Harris always took a special delight in tormenting and annoying his opponents. Upon leaving a port he would run alongside his rival, allowing passengers and crew to fling taunts at those aboard the slower craft. As the next port hove in sight, he would dash ahead and pick up the lion's share of the freight and passengers offered. . . .

The "Old Doctor," however, was almost a match for the *Dr. Franklin No. 2*, and so Captain Harris had to keep his new steamboat in fine trim in order to hold his advantage. Once, in May of 1851, while these two boats were engaged in tearing up the river bed in a port to port race to St. Paul, Captain Harris found himself hard pressed to maintain his lead. Indeed, when no freight or passengers were offered he was several times obliged to swing out the stage and discharge a willing and nimble passenger while his boat was moving under a slow bell.

Noting that his rival's boat lacked her usual speed, Captain M. W. Lodwick, rang for a full head of steam and momentarily threatened to pass the *Dr. Franklin No. 2*. Captain Harris frustrated these attempts at first by swinging the stern of his craft across the path of the "Old Doctor," forcing her to reverse to avoid a collision. Once the two boats almost crashed, skillful piloting and full speed astern on the part of the "Old Doctor" alone preventing a catastrophe. Incensed by these persistent and well-nigh successful attempts to wrest the lead from him, Captain Harris sprang from the pilot house to the hurricane deck brandishing a rifle, forced the pilot of the "Old Doctor" to back into the brush, and threatened to shoot if another attempt was made.

William J. Peterson, *Steamboating on the Upper Mississippi,* 1937

between St. Paul and Galena. Their much-heralded *Saint Paul,* "nearly the size of the Keokuk packets," failed to meet Smith Harris's expectations of speed, however. The *Saint Paul* was put on as a through boat to St. Louis and Harris went off to buy the sleek, fast, former St. Louis and Nashville packet *West Newton* to compete with *Nominee* on the Galena to St. Paul run, both boats making two trips a week.

Despite low water that forced out many boats as the season progressed, seventeen different steamboats logged a total of 171 arrivals in St. Paul in 1852. Thirteen of those arrivals were boats from the Minnesota River, where *Tiger, Black Hawk, Jenny Lind* and *Enterprise* were busy carrying settlers to their new homes on that river.

The Packet Companies Combine

Convinced that there was plenty of business for all if ruinous competition could be avoided, the two packet companies consolidated over the winter of 1852–53. Smith Harris became a director of the newly formed Galena and Minnesota Packet Company and Orrin Smith retired from the river to become the company's president. The combined line was able to put on four Galena packets, with a boat leaving Galena and St. Paul every day except Sunday. Thanks to Smith Harris's ability to find and buy excellent boats, the company rapidly expanded service and was able to keep rival lines from Keokuk and St. Louis from cutting into the upriver trade.

By 1852 **Nominee, Ben Campbell** and **Dr. Franklin** offered thrice-weekly service including the mail from Galena, and **Excelsior** was running every two weeks from St. Louis. "The Old Doctor" alone made 29 trips during the season. Advertisement from the *Weekly Minnesotian* (St. Paul) May 8, 1852.

Fast Boats Win the Customers

Smith Harris also won a kind of fame for the company by challenging the Keokuk Packet Line's *Die Vernon,* which was thought to be the fastest boat on western waters. In mid-June of 1853 the *Die* left St. Louis for St. Paul with an excursion party. At Galena she found Captain Harris lying in wait with the *West Newton.* Betting was heavy in Galena as Harris had bought up all the tar and rosin in that place to stoke his fires, and had made plain his intention of outstripping the *Die Vernon* or blowing up his boat in the process. When Captain Rufus Ford backed the

---

Competition Heats Up

The West Newton and the Nominee, both crowded with passengers, arrived at St. Paul Tuesday night, at about the same minute, in a strife all the way up. The old Nominee tucked up her petticoats and the way she did leg it through kept the West Newton at the top of her speed. We regret that this competition is reaching to such a pitch or in fact that it should reach *any* pitch. Let the lines both live and work at fair prices, without any such strife.

Minnesota Pioneer (St. Paul), July 22, 1852

St. Louis, Dubuque and St. Peter's Packet "Excelsior."

The first-class steamer EXCELSIOR, Jas. Ward, Master, having been thoroughly overhauled, repainted, &c., will run as a Regular Packet for the season, from St. Louis to Dubuque and St. Peters, and all intermediate landings. For freight or passage apply on board, or to

March 13, 1852.   G. R. WEST, Agent.

Dubuque and Galena Packet.

CAPTAIN ESTES has made arrangements for putting on this route the new and substantial steamer JENNY LIND, as soon as the opening of navigation will permit.

The Jenny is a first-class b iat of her size, and is perfectly new, having run only two months last autumn on Lake Winnebago. Her dimensions are 130 feet keel, and 24 beam, with two engines 16 inch cylinders, five feet stroke, and of very light draught.

February 24, 1852.   tf.

ARRANGEMENT

FOR   1852

GALENA AND MINNESOTA.

UNITED STATES MAIL LINE.

Consisting of *three first-class Boats:*
NOMINEE, Capt. O. Smith.
BEN CAMPBELL, Capt. M. W. Lodwick.
DR. FRANKLIN, Capt. R. Blakely.

Leaving Galena:

The NOMINEE, Capt. O. Smith, Mondays, at 12 o'clock.

The DR. FRANKLIN, Capt. R. Blakely, Wednesdays, at 12 o'clock.

The BEN CAMPBELL, Capt. M. W. Lodwick, Fridays, at 12 o'clock.

The above Boats will run regularly during the ensuing season. Having the Mail contract, their punctuality can be relied on. They will remain at St. Paul sufficiently long to enable passengers to visit the Falls of St. Anthony.

For speed and accommodations these boats are

The huge **Die Vernon** ran several excursions from St. Louis to St. Paul and the Falls of St. Anthony, and is remembered for her victorious race from Galena to St. Paul in July 1853 against the Galena and Minnesota Packet Company's **West Newton.** Her time was eighty-four hours, giving an average of 9½ miles per hour upstream. Drawing Missouri Historical Society, St. Louis.

Die Vernon out of Fever River the *West Newton* followed, "blowing off steam and making more noise than a stalled freight train."

Passing Dubuque, Harris gained the lead, but the *Die* was faster and slowly closed the gap until above La Crosse Harris landed the *West Newton* rather than be passed while under way. Harris took the defeat bitterly, arriving at and departing from St. Paul without leaving the hurricane deck.

It was left to Captain Orrin Smith and the company's other fast packet, *Nominee,* to avenge the defeat. While the excursionists were celebrating their victory at Maiden Rock, *Nominee* hove in sight and blew her challenge. *Nominee* led the *Die Vernon* all the way, and was last seen disappearing around the bend as the *Die* reached Dubuque and gave up the chase.

Such spirited competitions and individual boat's races against time were talked about up and down the Mississippi Valley. They made good business sense despite the dangers because passengers flocked to the fastest boats. The *West Newton's* race may have influenced the Rock Island Railroad promoters to choose the Galena and Minnesota Packet Company's boats for their celebrated excursion the following June.

The line packets stopped at many intermediate points, but it took many independent packets to fully serve the entire river. Transients such as *Asia* arrived at St. Paul in June 1853 "with a freight that would astonish." Her manifest showed that she had made stops at Quincy, Pontoosac, Dallas, Burlington, Muscatine, Davenport, Keithsburg, Albany, Savanna, Galena, Dubuque, Guttenberg, Clayton City, Prairie du Chien, Lansing, Wild Cat Bluffs, La Crosse,

---

Keeping to Schedules Is Not Always Easy

The Nominee was caught in a storm on Tuesday night and by being driven ashore, had one of her wheels badly crippled. She afterwards broke her rudder and lost 15 hours in repairing. To crown the chapter of accidents, she got aground yesterday afternoon near Kaposia [South St. Paul] where she lost several hours. These unlucky incidents explain why she was from Monday till late on Thursday night making the trip up.

Minnesotian (St. Paul), July 15, 1854

Hammond's Landing, Nelson's Landing, Prescott and Stillwater. In addition, dozens of smaller boats carried on local trades, shuttling back and forth between not-too-far-distant ports.

Other steamers that kept to a regular timetable were the St. Louis to St. Paul packets *Excelsior* and *Grand Prairie,* the first Minnesota-owned packet *Greek Slave,* and two Minnesota

River stalwarts, *Clarion* and *Black Hawk.*

During 1853 St. Paul logged 235 steamboat arrivals, 94 of them made by the Minnesota Packet Company's four boats. Forty-nine boats arrived from the Minnesota River, which was fast becoming an important route for settlers moving west. By 1854 there were fourteen packets providing regular service from Galena to St. Paul, at least twenty more that made occasional trips, and a dozen or so plying the Minnesota, St. Croix and Wisconsin rivers. Several steamers wintered over above Lake Pepin to be ready to operate on the upper river in the spring before the boats from below could penetrate the lake ice.

Railroads Fuel Packet Line Expansion . . . for a Time

As regularly scheduled railroads reached the Mississippi, the steamboat business increased. For the first few years the traffic generated by the railroads was so heavy there were not steamboats enough to carry it on. This gave advantage to the packet companies, as the railroads often refused to deal with independents; they preferred to cooperate with the regular lines because they could offer through bills of lading, and often had joint agents in the river towns.

Soon after the Chicago and Rock Island Railroad reached Rock Island in 1854 a new packet line—the Rock Island Mail Line—began running between Rock Island and Galena. St. Louis merchants organized the Northern Line

The Galena & Minnesota Packet Co. boat **Nominee** at Galena c. 1852. The popular **Nominee** was a temperance boat that served no liquor. Her pious captain, Orrin Smith, would not run on Sundays and allowed no card playing. Photo Minnesota Historical Society.

Packet Company in 1854, using eight boats between St. Louis and St. Paul. When the Illinois Central Railroad reached Dunleith in 1855, the Galena and Minnesota Packet Company shifted operations to Dubuque, just across the river from the railhead, and reorganized as the Galena, Dunleith and Minnesota Packet Company. This company continued to expand to provide connections with the new railheads at Prairie du Chien and La Crosse.

A third packet line began at La Crosse in 1860, run by the shrewd William F. Davidson and supported by the La Crosse and Milwaukee Railroad. Davidson's La Crosse and St. Paul Packet Company became the active rival of the older upper river companies, eventually absorbing them all.

The expansion spurred by the railroads also affected the economies of river towns in between. Woodyards stockpiling fuel for steamboats sprang up along the riverbanks and many river communities became home to boatyards and drydocks.

As steamboats became profitable ventures, many were owned by individuals and firms in upriver communities who used them as local packets, fueling the growth of settlement on the smaller rivers. As early as 1855 the merchants of St. Paul were discussing establishment of their own packet line to Dunleith and Rock Island to "break down the monopoly of the Galena Packet Company." But as the railroads continued to advance west, the service they offered proved to be more efficient than that offered by the steamboats, and the packet business gradually faded away. By the end of the Civil War, the steamboating boom had come and gone on the Upper Mississippi.

CHAPTER EIGHT

A Wonderful Flow
of Commodities

The western riverboat was first of all a freight carrier. In the early years, the steamboat was most useful for its ability to carry goods upstream rapidly and cheaply. Cargos were manufactured items, chiefly clothing, and groceries such as flour, beans, coffee, salt beef and pork destined for military establishments along the river. Passengers were a secondary consideration, except for the troops and officials connected to the military.

On the Upper Mississippi there was little cargo available for the return trip, the chief commodities being furs and buffalo robes gathered by licensed traders during the winters and shipped to their St. Louis depots each spring. The American Fur Company got into the steamboat business to assure reliable transportation for Indian trade goods going into the backcountry and valuable furs coming out.

Fur Company consignments consisted of trade items imported from the American East and Europe—blankets, cloth, earbobs and other ornaments, cooking pots, hunting equipment including guns, knives and traps—that would be traded to the Indians for furs and skins. More significant to the steamboat owners were the bulk commodities—the barrels of pork, flour, sugar, salt, gunpowder and liquor—that constituted the biggest portion of most shipments. These commodities were products of the Missisippi and Ohio river valleys, supplied by local merchants and farmers.

Furs and buffalo hides, the latter in great demand for carriage robes, came from as far away as the Red River valley, Canada and the Dakota plains. They were hauled to St. Paul in trains

Two-wheeled ox carts, shown here creaking through the village of St. Anthony with the falls in the background, carried furs and buffalo robes from the Red River Valley to waiting steamboats at St. Paul. Daguerreotype c. 1854, Minnesota Historical Society.

of two-wheeled ox carts to be shipped back East on steamboats.

Government shipping remained far more important than private commerce on the upper river until the 1850s. Steamboats were an efficient way to transport military supplies and troops to frontier posts. They were also hired to transport the commissioners and Indian delegations to the treaty grounds and, ultimately, to remove whole bands to their new homes on reservations. The yearly delivery of annuity payments to the Indian bands became a rich source of revenue to local businesses as well as to steamboat owners. In 1839 *Pizarro* was noted carrying 20 spinning wheels, 20 looms, 300 axes, 100 plows and $10,000 in coin to the Iowa Indians. Another manifest shows *Fire Canoe* with two barges containing several tons of flour, pork, lard and corn going up the Minnesota to the Dakota Indian agency near Redwood Falls.

Lead Spurs Traffic on the Upper River

If one commodity could be said to have attracted steamboats to the Mississippi above the Des Moines rapids, that commodity would be lead. Lead was being dug and shipped by barge and keelboat from Dubuque and Galena at the beginning of the nineteenth century. The coming of steamboats to the upper river in the 1820s

The 79-ton tramp steamer **Excel** is shown with three barges and a flatboat in tow. Even a small steamboat such as **Excel** could move a large freight by towing barges. This boat arrived at Stillwater from Le Claire, Iowa, in 1854 with 1,192 bushels of corn. Photo Murphy Library, University of Wisconsin–La Crosse.

hastened the industry's development. Lead mining brought thousands of adventurous settlers to the Upper Mississippi, which created a demand for a supply line of steamboats to Galena, Dubuque and Potosi, the outlets for the mines. The stampede for the Fever River lead mines began in 1827, and soon Galena boasted a population of thousands. As more boats steamed north to pick up the lucrative lead ore they brought more settlers to Galena. By the mid-1830s thirty boats were running regularly in the lead trade, and by 1848 a quarter of the steamboats docking at St. Louis had come from upriver, the majority from Galena, Potosi, Cassville and Dubuque.

Many captains were willing to risk their boats on the rapids for the enormous returns that could be reaped by transporting lead. In 1848 alone the value of lead shipped to St. Louis was $1.6 million, five times the value of furs from the Mississippi and Missouri rivers combined! In today's money, that would be about $36 million.

Keelboats and Barges Increase Steamers' Capacity

Many steamboats towed keelboats to increase their carrying capacity. The keels also provided some protection for the steamer, as a "tow" was always pushed ahead of the boat and would therefore find the sharp-fanged rock first. In 1839 the sidewheeler *Ione* left Galena for St. Louis towing three keels loaded with 400 tons of lead—such a cargo might pay for the steamboat in one trip! Flat-bottomed barges began to turn up on the Upper Mississippi in the mid-1820s and by 1850 they had replaced the keelboat in

tows.

Safety barges, which placed the passenger quarters on a separate barge towed by the steamboat, were introduced in the late 1820s

A Gentle Caution for Shippers

We have many hardships to encounter and are exposed to many dangers, which of course we submit to without a murmur, but we would respectfully request our friends not to heap upon us, through their *kindness,* more than we can conveniently endure.

Now, *a short story at a woodpile.* On loading my boat at a place of this kind last trip, I discovered several black marks upon the deck, which, on examination, I found to be gunpowder, from a box which my men were about to store away as dry goods, which in part did contain dry goods, but in the middle concealed, was a considerable quantity of powder, so carelessly placed, that it was strewn throughout the package. Now, I have only to request that whenever any of my customers have powder to ship, that they will not conceal it, and thereby endanger our lives, but inform us of it. . . . It is not my wish to complain, but it is my wish to run my boat with as much safety as possible; and I trust this gentle caution will be attended to.

Captain Joseph Throckmorton, notice in St. Louis *Missouri Republican,* July 12, 1833

primarily because there were so many steamboat boiler explosions. The safety barge not only protected passengers from what was perceived as the worst danger of steamboats, but also allowed the steamer to run lightly loaded in low water. Steamboat owners soon learned that spreading the load on shallow-draft barges enabled them

Captain G. W. Atchison commanded **Amaranth** in the St. Louis–Galena–Prairie du Chien trade and also on the St. Croix River. Her profitability was greatly enhanced by towing two large barges. After being stranded in 1842, she was rebuilt and continued a stalwart in the Galena lead trade through 1846. Photo collection of Mrs. J. Long, copy in Murphy Library, University of Wisconsin–La Crosse.

packets. The 147-foot steamer towed two 140-foot open-hold barges, the first of the type, that had been built especially to be towed alongside her. These barges gave her an amazing cargo capacity. In May 1843 she was logged leaving Galena crowded with passengers and carrying one of the biggest freights ever seen, which included 13,000 pigs of lead weighing 455 tons. Of course the down side was that there was a bigger cargo to lose; when *Amaranth* was stranded on the Mississippi in late 1842, boat and cargo suffered a $15,575 loss—worth today over $300,000.

Steamboats Supply the Lumber Camps

Through the 1840s and 1850s, lumbering companies in the Chippewa and St. Croix valleys hired men by the hundreds to work in the pineries. Boatloads of German and Irish immigrants were recruited in St. Louis for work in the woods at $12 a month. The more men in the pineries, the more supplies were needed to be shipped in after them. Many of the boats destined for Gilbert's and Nelson's Landings on Lake Pepin and Stillwater on the St. Croix were filled with goods for upriver lumber camps. Besides the flour, pork, coffee, tea and sugar that were required to feed hungry lumberjacks, cargoes contained nails, stovepipe, candles, turpentine, harness, rope and buckshot.

In 1851 *Hindoo* had a mill and millstones for Taylor & Fox at Taylors Falls on her deck; others brought circular and crosscut saws, broad

to pass the rapids more successfully. Heavily laden boats still had to rely on lighting—that is, offloading cargo onto flatboats—to get past the rapids, a costly and time-consuming process.

In 1841 Captain George W. Atchison entered the upper Mississippi trade with *Amaranth,* at 220 tons one of the bigger upper-river

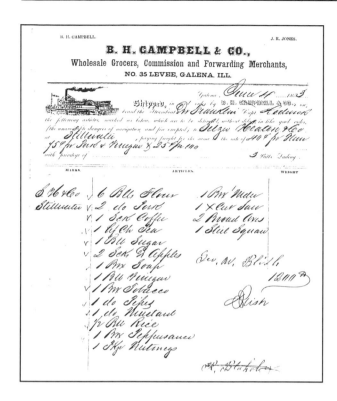

axes, blacksmith bellows and iron, grindstones, bedsteads and mattresses—even a skiff and a boat anchor—to St. Croix ports.

Late-season boats laden with winter supplies were anxiously awaited. Goods shipped on *Prairie Bird* to the St. Croix River at the end of October 1847 included fourteen dozen wool socks and two kegs of lard. Captains willing to brave the November ice pack might charge a premium for the run, but the cost was still less than freighting goods overland after the freeze-up. Probably also destined for the lumber companies, who were the big employers on the St. Croix, was a *Montauk* cargo that included 1,259 pounds of drugs consigned to forwarding agents Churchill & Nelson at Stillwater.

This bill of lading from Galena wholesalers shows a cargo that contained pipes, tobacco, soap, pepper sauce, mustard and apples as well as staple foods and tools needed in a lumber camp. They were brought up on the **Dr. Franklin** and consigned to Setzer, Heaton & Co. at Stillwater. Merrick papers, State Historical Society of Wisconsin.

The medium-sized packet **Cora,** shown here at Taylors Falls on the St. Croix, was able to deliver supplies to the mill company warehouse at the head of navigation in periods of high water. Oil painting, "Gorge of the St. Croix," by Henry Lewis, 1847. Minneapolis Institute of Arts, The Julia B. Bigelow Fund.

Most items destined for the mills on the St. Croix were off-loaded at Stillwater where forwarding agents sent them on by keelboat or one of the small packets that plied the river. When they were in a hurry or when the water was low, larger boats would put off their cargoes for the St. Croix at Prescott, situated on the Mississippi at the outlet of Lake St. Croix.

Goods left at Stillwater or Prescott were often reshipped on the smaller packets—*Humboldt, Enterprise, Montello* and the minuscule 40-foot *Queen of the Yellow Banks*—that from 1851 through 1855 provided several-times-a-week service up the St. Croix River. Because of the possibility they might not get through to their destination, most packets only accepted freight with the privilege of "lighting, towing, reshipping and storing in case of ice [or low water] at the owner's risk and expense."

Some cargos may have suffered by being handled so many times; for example, a note dated August of 1854 shows the Schulenberg Mill on Lake St. Croix received goods from the *Julia Dean* "in bad order on board the *Black Hawk*." Other steamers got their cargos to the destination themselves. Incredible as it may seem today, in high water even larger side-wheelers such as *Cora, Excelsior* and *Indian Queen* might make it through to St. Croix Falls.

Tombstones, Mail and Other Necessities

As miners, lumbermen and settlers arrived in the Upper Mississippi valley, following the route established by the early steamboats from St. Louis, the demand for supplies increased. The boats already in the lead trade started to carry furniture, paint, kettles, ploughs, cradles, trunks, clothing and other merchandise wanted in the rapidly expanding frontier towns. Upbound steamboat cargos frequently included livestock as well as manufactured goods and, occasionally, bulk commodities.

Bills of lading show that *Argo* arrived at Stillwater in May of 1847 with a cookstove, boiler and stovepipe on board. In 1848 the *Dr.*

First Steamboat Arrival.

Last evening, about eight o'clock, a steamboat was distinctly heard, four or five miles below, and the whole town was instantly agog. In a few minutes the familiar whistle of the *Nominee* was heard just around the point, which was soon drowned by the shouts of the elated citizens. Presently she made the landing amid the deafening cheers of all St. Paul and those on board. Capt. [Orrin] Smith informs us that he had much difficulty in getting through the ice. The lake [Pepin] is not yet broken up, and he had to take advantage of a favorable gust of wind, which drove it across the lake, while the boat crowded up along shore.

Weekly Minnesotian (St. Paul), April 17, 1852

There were few wharves on the Mississippi because of fluctuating water levels. Space at the landing was often at a premium, so old steamboat hulls were moored as wharfboats that served as floating docks and warehouses. Shown with a wharfboat at an unknown location are the steamboats **Des Moines** and **Emerald** c.1862. Murphy Library, University of Wisconsin—La Crosse.

Franklin brought up two bobsleds, four head of cattle and a quantity of feed oats. And in 1854 *Navigator* was freighted with 380 pounds of marble, consigned to Short & Proctor at Stillwater and no doubt destined for tombstones.

Bringing the News from "Below"

Throughout the 1830s and 1840s steamboats were often first to bring news from the rest of the country to ice-locked settlements on the northern river. For example, Minnesotans did not know they were living in the new Territory of Minnesota for over a month until the first boat of the season, *Dr. Franklin No. 2*, arrived in April 1849 carrying Henry Sibley home from Washington, D.C., with the news.

Boats also carried the mail and newspapers, which were eagerly awaited each spring by news-starved St. Paulites who often saw no mail for four to five months over the winter. Until the middle 1850s, when regular mail service was established to St. Paul, any boat leaving for that port might carry the mail sack. Because mail service was sporadic, for years most letters were carried by passengers. Steamboat clerks frequently brought up the newspapers, and some would even undertake to deliver small packages as a service to their customers.

At St. Paul the first steamboat arrival each year was a memorable occasion. Townspeople flocked to the levee to greet the boat, no matter if it were the middle of the night or a pouring rainstorm. The boat's bar did a roaring business as townspeople rushed aboard, and the passengers sometimes found it difficult to get themselves and their baggage off the boat.

FANCY GOODS—China and alabaster Flower Vases plain and figured, Bohemian Colognes, Card Baskets, Cigar holders, China card Baskets, fine China Inks, alabaster paper weights, Ladies Rosewood work boxes, Gentlemen's Dressing Cases, Chess men from $2.50 to $40.00 per sett, and many other things in our line. For sale by LE DUC & ROHRER

FRESH ARRIVAL OF GROCERIES

At Wholesale & Retail,

[NEXT DOOR TO THE WORLD'S FAIR ON ROBERTS ST.]

REY & FARMER have just received by the Nominee, one of the most extensive and best selected assortment of Groceries ever before received in Minnesota, which they will sell at a small advance for cash. They wish it distinctly understood that they have no Liquor on hand, do not expect any, nor wish to deal in it. Among the leading articles which we shall offer, will be, (besides every other kind of goods usually found in a large grocery establishment, whether here enumerated or not,) the following:

Flour, of various brands;
Sugar & Molasses, of all kinds;
Coffee, Tea, Tobacco, Salt, Salt Fish, Oysters, Sardines, Butter, Cheese, Lard and Oil.
Provisions: consisting of Pork, Hams, Bacon, Dried Fruit, etc.
Patent buckets, Glass, Nails, Putty, Shot, Matches, Candles, Soap, Brushes, Brooms, and a great variety of other goods.
12 bbls. Hydraulic Cement.
St. Paul, April 1852. 32-y

FRESH LEMONS—5 boxes just received per Caleb Cope, and for sale by REY & FARMER.

CARPET WARP—A large quantity just arrived and for sale by REY & FARMER.

DEMIJOHNS—150, 1, 2, 3, 4 and 5 galls, received per Excelsior, and for sale by H F M'CLOSKEY.

COFFEE—350 bags Rio coffee just received per Golden Era, and for sale by H F M'CLOSKEY.

TOBACCO—125 bxs. Virginia, rec'd and for sale by H F M'CLOSKEY.

FIGS—500 drums received and for sale by H F M'CLOSKEY.

RICE—25 tierces rec'd per Golden Era and for sale by H F M'CLOSKEY.

SALERATUS—25 bxs. Boston Saleratus, rec'd and for sale by H F M'CLOSKEY.

MACKEREL—75 bbls. No. 1, 2 and 3 mackerel, rec'd per Golden Era, and for sale by H F M'CLOSKEY.

TEA—150 hf. chests G. P. Imp. and Y H tea rec'd p r Golden Era, and for sale by H F M'CLOSKEY.

FINE assortme
GOOD assortm by
DOZ canisters sale by
CASES best Chewing Toba
DOZ Brooms, f
O. Sugar, Cl ed do. for s
BEST Rio Coff
BBLS. best 5 do Pale C 1 4 cask sup 2 bbls each deira Wines, in st
WILL take a country in pay prices.
1500 bushels 500 do 500 do For goods at lo
MINNESOTA Received per st our counter, also by Chu H. C. Folsom, Taylor's F Rapids. May 8.
AMERICAN Received and for
WRAPING P Double Crown o Wholesale Prices.
WALL PAPE assortment by
LIFE OF JO Roanoke, by Hu Bookstore of
THE ARABIA tainments, Transl reading, and illustrated

Advertisements show the variety of goods available to citizens of St. Paul in the 1850s, including fresh lemons brought by the first steamboats of the season. *Daily Minnesotian* (St. Paul), May 8, 1852.

When several boats came in together, each striving to be first, pandemonium reigned on the levee where tons of freight were dumped willy-nilly. Dozens of carters hovered about with their horses and drays, looking for customers and freight to haul. Steamboat races got started because captains knew that the first boat into any port would get the best pick of the cargo available. Likewise, the first boat to a woodyard would get the choice dry fuel.

St. Paul newspapers reveal the vast selection of merchandise available to people of the Northwest, thanks to the steamboats. In April 1852 the Saint Anthony Store (located opposite the falls in the Mississippi) advertised dry goods and family groceries including Java, Rio and St. Domingo coffee, chocolate, cocoa, black tea, ginger, cassia, mustard and other spices, raisins, currants and dried peaches. The store also carried personal needs such as snuff, chewing and smoking tobacco and household products as varied as saleratus (baking powder), starch, soap, indigo and "confectionery of all kinds." And it stocked a vast array of household goods including hardware, irons, coffee mills, looking glasses, crockery, combs, dyes, paints, turpentine, clocks and a "lot of Yankee notions." Just about anything available in St. Louis was by the 1850s available at St. Paul and other upper river towns.

Commodities Going Downstream

In the 1850s the flow of bulk commodities

This stereograph view of the St. Paul levee shows produce waiting to be loaded for shipment downstream. Grain was shipped in two-bushel sacks, easy to handle and convenient for stowing on steamboats. Other commodities such as flour, salt, crackers, dried fish, meat and whiskey traveled in barrels. Zimmerman photo c. 1865. Minnesota Historical Society.

Potosi with 4,600 sacks of wheat plus oats and corn, *Lamartine* had arrived from Dubuque freighted with potatoes, flour and corn, and *Editor* has arrived from St. Paul with corn,

Sights and Sounds on a Steamboat

All the steamers carry freight, that being, indeed, their principal business and source of profit, to which the accommodation of passengers (as far as time is concerned), has to stand secondary. We . . . picked up all sorts of goods from all sorts of places [and] took in what would have been considered a very fair cargo to a New York liner. At one place, for instance, we shipped several hundred barrels of pork; ditto of lard; at another place, an uncounted (by me) lot of flour. . . . Besides these we had bags of coffee, rolls of leather, groceries, dry goods, hardware, all sorts of agricultural products, innumerable coops filled with live geese, turkeys, and fowls, that kept up a perpetual farmyard concert. . . . To my eyes it was enormous, though people much used to such things didn't seem to consider it any wonder at all.

Walt Whitman, 1848, "Excerpts from a Traveller's Note Book," in Emory Halloway, ed., *The Uncollected Poetry and Prose of Walt Whitman,* 1921

began to reverse itself. Whereas earlier boats had brought feed grains such as oats and corn upriver to the lumber camps, by the early years of the decade quantities of agricultural products began to find their way down the Mississippi. Iowa, Wisconsin and Minnesota farmers planted wheat, which was sacked over the winter for shipping to southern and eastern markets.

The first boats through to St. Paul in the spring got the bulk of the waiting produce, many returning to St. Louis so loaded their guards were "partly sunk." St. Louis newspapers reported in one week of May 1854 that *Hindoo* was in from

wheat, butter, oats, barley and bacon and four boxes of gold—a $230,000 cargo (worth $4.9 million today!).

Ice was another reliable northland commodity. Bargeloads of ice cut over the winter and packed in sawdust were towed to southern ports each spring to provide the necessity for lemonade and mint juleps before the advent of refrigeration.

Other commodities shipped downstream, especially in the fall, included cranberries, salt meat, turnips, beets, onions, hay and whiskey. Because they kept so well, cranberries were in demand from the 1840s on. These wild fruits grew throughout the swampy areas of Minnesota and Wisconsin and were often harvested by Indian women, as well as by local settlers for the additional income. In September 1849 the *Minnesota Chronicle* reported that 2,135 barrels of cranberries had already been shipped from St. Paul and Mendota. Before the season was over several more boats had departed St. Paul freighted with 400 or 500 barrels each!

Among the more unusual cargoes ever loaded at St. Paul was a live buffalo bull (American bison), sent in 1853 to the Crystal Palace Exhibition held in New York City. Minnesota's display, meant to help develop a market for Minnesota agricultural products, included wild rice, wheat from Cottage Grove, furs from Mendota and, as an attention-getter, the semi-tame young buffalo that had been trained to pull a sled.

The animal was loaded on the *Ben Franklin* at St. Paul, transferred at Galena and St. Louis to other steamers, and at Cincinnati placed on a train for Albany, New York. The poor beast got such bad treatment on the journey that by the time he reached New York City he was quite wild and charged the judges who were assembling the exhibit. Needless to say, he was rejected as an item of display, and was finally sold to a showman.

CHAPTER NINE

Migrants, Immigrants and Fugitive Slaves

I t was natural for steamboats to handle freight and passengers together. The earlier boats had no specific passenger accommodations, but those hauling freight might charge a premium to take passengers in their small deck cabin. Others made room for passengers on the deck with the freight, where they required little attention from the crew. Some travelers paid for their passage by helping to wood the boat.

Packets Become All-Purpose Carriers

At the height of the shipping seasons (spring and fall), when they were heavily loaded, some boats would not stop on hail or put in at small settlements along the way for freight or passengers. But most captains who owned their own boats would stop to take any business that might come their way. Through the 1840s, except for government charters, few boats made the full trip from St. Louis to the St. Peters. Most steamboats worked only what the captain considered to be a profitable section of the river, so travelers ordinarily had to use two or three steamboats to reach a distant port. They made their own arrangements as they found boats available, and few knew when they started out

Passenger tickets for the **Die Vernon, Mansfield** and **Minnesota Belle.** These boats were popular passenger packets advertised from St. Louis to St. Paul in the early 1850s. Battle of Lexington State Historic Site, Lexington, Missouri.

how they would arrive at their destination. Freight shippers who could not find a through boat would have to arrange for the cargo to be forwarded, hence the large number of consignment warehouses and forwarding agents in river towns. The system involved considerable delay and expense.

As boats grew bigger, the cabin quarters were shifted to the upper deck to make more cargo space below. This kept passengers out of the way and also made their life more pleasant. On early two-deckers there were generally two cabins, one at the rear (away from the boilers and smokestacks) for the ladies and one at the front for the gentlemen, both lined with berths that could be curtained off from the main room. When separate staterooms became common, the two cabins were turned into one large salon and dining hall, although the ladies always retained a private place at the rear. By the early 1840s open berths were a thing of the past and the race was on to woo passengers with ever more elegant quarters.

The Competition for Passengers

The passenger business expanded as packet line service came into being. Line boats advertised through tickets for passengers, promising that they would meet the ongoing boat and transfer passengers and baggage without delay. Passengers, unlike freight shippers, cared what kind of boat they traveled on so, although all steamboats carried passengers, the bulk of the business fell to the newest, largest and most luxurious vessels.

Cabin fare at first was expensive, but as competition heated up, the fares came down, except in periods of exceptionally low water and at the very start and end of the season. By

The **Golden Era** was a fast and luxurious steamer that carried Ex-president Millard Fillmore on the Grand Excursion. By the 1860s she was a railroad packet, moving freight and passengers from Dunleith to St. Paul. Behind her in this picture is a Civil War gunboat. Photo taken c.1863. State Historical Society of Wisconsin.

1848 one could travel from Galena to St. Paul in a comfortable cabin (with all meals) for $5 to $6, or on deck (no meals) for $2.50. Freight went the same distance at 25¢ per hundredweight, horses and cattle at $4 a head. By comparison, travel by train from Buffalo to Chicago cost a passenger $10 and the stage ride from Chicago to Galena was $8 more, with no food and lodging provided. (You can multiply 1848 prices by twenty to approximate today's cost.)

As already noted, when there was intense competition, fares might drop to ruinous rates. To save money and provide the fastest service, certain captains were known to get a bit parsimonious. In 1845, while Smith Harris was setting speed records with his *War Eagle,* some passengers became dissatisfied that during the 44-hour trip from St. Louis to Galena only one dinner had been served. The captain pointed out that the *War Eagle* had left after noon on Tuesday and reached Galena before noon on Thursday, so only Wednesday dinner could be served. He also informed the grumblers that if they were traveling for dinners they would have to take a slower boat.

The Passenger Experience

The floating population was quite diverse, combining people from all classes of society and all parts of the world and throwing them together in one noisy, cramped riverboat. On the whole the passengers on most boats were well behaved. However, certain behaviors were frowned upon. Posted regulations forbade "gentlemen" to lie down in berths with their boots on, to appear coatless at meals, to enter the ladies' cabin without consent, to smoke in the salon, to whittle or otherwise injure the furniture, and so on.

Table manners were often called into question. One passenger in 1841 wrote: "When the supper bell rang what a rush . . . and such a clatter of knives and forks and tableware, such screaming for waiters, . . . such an exhibition of

Scene on the Galena Landing

The variety of faces and the varieties of expression furnish food for many a thoughtful suggestion. The stalwart lumberman from Maine, the thrifty and sharp trader from the land of steady habits, the hardy independent mechanic from the Empire State, the phlegmatic Hollander, the philosophical German, the wily scheming politician, full of thoughts of future preferment—all at times accompanied by hopeful trusting woman, who goes to share the fate of those to whom her life is bound by "hooks of triple steel," often jostle each other for the first time, here, on this last resting place between the crowded East and the wide and virgin North West. Here emigrants lay in their supplies for a new home. The loaded drays that crowd the street, are filled with articles as numerous and as different as the hopes, or the motives, of those for whose comfort or sustenance they are intended. . . . All, like the owners, are stowed together. . . . The word Contentment is not in their vocabulary.

Jeffersonian (Galena), Oct. 25, 1851

On a Mississippi Riverboat, June 11, 1837

This was not the first time that I had had the bad luck to find myself on board one of the numerous class of low, dirty steamers that ply on the Mississippi. Those of the first class are noble vessels, clean, comfortable, generally well commanded and provided with every thing necessary and nothing permitted on board that can be reasonably objected to. The Envoy was one of a class of disreputable steamers, not seaworthy, usually commanded by low, drunken fellows, who run about from place to place, picking up freight and chance passengers amongst the coarse dissipated gamblers that abound on the western rivers and frontiers . . . Many of these fellows live on board, and are the colleagues of the captain in various kinds of villainy They are eternally playing at a low game of cards, called poker, sleeping two or three hours in the daytime. . . .

During the confusion on board I had kept as near the stern as I could, seated on a large, loose bench, which, in the expectation that we should explode, and that I might have to float myself ashore, promised to be of some use; fortunately, perhaps, we ran aground after midnight, and remained stuck fast until near five in the morning. In this Pandemonium, how many of our passengers and crew were drunk, and how it came to pass that we were not blown up or set fire to, was not explained to me.

George W. Featherstonhaugh, *A Canoe Voyage Up the Minnay Sotor,* 2

practices. Plenty of male passengers became bored with the slow progress of the boat and passed the time in drinking and card playing. Travelers often carried large amounts of money and presented "easy pickin's" for professional gamblers. Blacklegs, short-card artists, three-card monte throwers and other sharpers were common on riverboats and hard to get rid of as they generally paid their full fare and were good liberal customers at the bar. Sometimes, also, they were in cahoots with the management.

On the larger and finer steamboats, especially those advertising excursions, passengers had a different experience. Many travelers' accounts praise the table settings, the perfectly trained waiters, and the elaborate meals formally served with after-dinner music provided by the boat's band. Those who secured passage on Orrin Smith's *Nominee,* a deservedly popular temperance boat, were usually happy to find no liquor was served and Sundays were strictly kept. However, it must be said this kind of accommodation was not standard on Upper Mississippi riverboats.

Steamboats stopped for freight and passengers often and as many as six times a day to wood up. Each time a boat stopped at a settlement, vendors would throng the boat selling chestnuts and apples, newspapers and books. On these occasions passengers were free to walk about on shore and take in the local sights and this, along with music, dancing, conversation and promenades on the boiler deck, was sufficient to keep most travelers amused, or even

muscle and nerve. . . . The table was cleared in an amazing short space of time and food was *bolted* as I have never seen before."

Drinking and gambling were two pursuits that were well established on most riverboats, even those whose captains tried to abolish the

mildly excited. Others found the journey, especially if a long one, monotonous in the extreme. Wrote one discouraged passenger: "Three meals a day—reading a little, talking a little, walking a little, and all the while paddle, paddle, puff."

"Go West, Young Man, Go West!"

These words, popularly attributed to Horace Greeley of the New York *Tribune*, were actually written in 1851 by John Soule, an Indiana newspaperman. By then, the restless American public had little need of his advice. They were already on the move. A decade before, in 1841, Greeley himself had promoted western settlement by exhorting people crowded into Eastern cities: "If you have no family or friends to aid you, turn your face to The Great West and there build up your home and fortune."

A Nation of Movers

Through the 1830s and '40s thousands of families left their homes in New England and New York to travel to the Mississippi Valley. They usually came by way of the Great Lakes to Chicago, then overland to Galena where they dispersed north and west.

Frequent stops to take on firewood provided passengers with a welcome diversion. So many used the opportunity to take a drink that "to wood" became a euphemistic term for "to take a dram." The Steamboat "Grand Turk" Wooding at Night, lithograph by Henry Lewis c. 1850 from *Das Illustrirte Mississippithal*.

St. Paul's bustling lower levee on the Mississippi could be a scene of utter chaos when several steamboats arrived at once. Carters and coaches awaited the chance to transport goods and passengers inland. Lithograph from Map of City of St. Paul 1857, Minnesota Historical Society.

even noted arriving at St. Paul with the materials of a house, framed and prepared for immediate erection. These "prefabs" were popular on the frontier, where there was usually a shortage of both materials and craftsmen.

A Deluge of Immigrants Into Minnesota Territory

Immigration took off with the establishment of Minnesota Territory in 1849. When the Dakota bands relinquished their lands in southern Minnesota in 1851, the packet companies found it hard to keep up with the flood of emigrants. Even before the treaties were ratified, the rush of settlers to Minnesota had begun; in 1851 Galena newspapers noted a 300 percent increase in freight and passenger traffic bound for Minnesota and predicted, "Minnesota will treble her population the present summer." The *Minnesota Democrat* reported that the *Lamartine* had been offered three times as much as she could carry at Galena.

There was a heavy influx of emigrants from the eastern United States into northern Iowa and western Wisconsin as well. Between 1852 and 1857 steamboat arrivals at St. Paul quintupled, and by the mid-1850s passenger traffic had

Thousands more from the mid-Atlantic states and Pennsylvania traveled by covered wagon to the Mississippi valley, sometimes settling first in Ohio and Kentucky before moving on. Those who could afford it made their entire journey by steamboat, first on the Ohio, then the Mississippi River.

Some pioneer American families traveled crowded onto steamboats as deckers with their entire families plus household stuff, pots, kettles, cattle and dogs and "all the paraphernalia of the backwoods farm." In 1849 several families were

Western steamboat travel as caricatured in the Eastern press. The conditions and dangers of steamboat travel were easy to exaggerate. From a lithograph in *Harpers New Monthly Magazine*, 1858.

Western Steamboat, with full cargo.

A Hot Boat.—Ten 56lbs. weights on safety-valve

Running on a Bank.

VOL. XVIII.

superseded freight as the most profitable cargo for steamboats.

Many emigrants traveled in companies, pooling their resources to enable them to buy land and build a settlement in the west. In 1851 *Wyoming* brought up several boatloads of Germans, one group of which was planning to establish a socialist community at El Kader (now Elkader, Iowa). Other group settlements were established at Zumbrota, Garden City and Excelsior, Minnesota.

These colonizers were usually well organized and quite well to do; some even hired their own steamboats. Often an agent of the settlers' company came first to seek out the best site for the colony and purchase the land. Then the members of the company would arrive with everything needed to lay out and build a town. They moved and resettled as communities, and were ready to resume their accustomed relationships very quickly.

Others were not so well organized and were ripe for swindlers. In the spring of 1852, members of the Western Farm and Village Association of New York City arrived on the *Nominee* from Galena to settle on their purchased lands in Rolling Stone, Minnesota. They had with them a beautiful birds-eye view map of the place showing the library, hotels, a lecture hall and warehouses and they expected to be put off at the city dock.

But there was no such place as Rolling

Emigrant routes to the Upper Mississippi. "Yankees" and "Yorkers," from New England and downstate New York, tended to follow the Great Lakes route. Those from Pennsylvania and the mid-Atlantic states generally came by wagon train or Ohio River steamboat to St. Louis. Some European emigrants entered the U.S. at New Orleans, using an all-water route. Foreign emigrants settled disproportionately in urban areas; the ethnic heritage is still strong in places such as Chicago, Milwaukee, St. Louis and St. Paul.

Stone, and at last they were put ashore at the mouth of Rollingstone Creek few miles above Wabasha Prairie to fend for themselves. Not being farmers, they were unequal to the task of building houses and opening farms, and when winter set in the Rolling Stone Colony was virtually abandoned, although some of its members went on to found Minnesota City.

Unfortunately, hundreds of "town-site sharks" flourished along the river between Dunleith and St. Paul, and many would-be settlers unwisely invested their money without seeing the property that was so glowingly promoted back East.

Most of the foreign-born who came to America and the Upper Mississippi Valley between 1830 and 1854 used the steamboat for all or part of their journey, often traveling first to New Orleans, then up the Mississippi. Germans predominated and by 1849 already formed a large population in St. Louis, southern Wisconsin and many Iowa river towns, and soon were moving into southeastern Minnesota and the Minnesota River valley.

There was also a sizable population from the British Isles and Canada and, during the 1850s in Minnesota especially, extensive immigration from Sweden and other Scandinavian countries. Stillwater on the St. Croix River became an important point of arrival for Swedes, as well as the depot for lumbering supplies going into the pineries, with two or more boats arriving weekly in 1851.

Steamboats Promote Settlement on Rivers

It stands to reason that some steamboat captains would catch speculative fever as well. Captain Orrin Smith of Galena had watched the incoming tide of immigration and realized that Wabasha Prairie (site of Winona) in Minnesota was an ideal location for a city that could supply settlements in the interior.

With the treaties not yet ratified, in October 1851 Smith landed Erwin H. Johnson at night from the *Nominee* with two men, ostensibly wood-choppers, who were to aid Johnson in occupying the claim. A month later several more claimants recruited by Smith appeared on *Excelsior*. Rather than fight over the landing sites, the parties staked out the waterfront in one-half mile sections and then chose them alternately. The original plat of Winona was surveyed in June 1852 for Erwin H. Johnson and Orrin Smith.

Captain Samuel Humberstone also noticed the success of certain townsite speculators. In early 1854 he bought the well-furnished packet *Minnesota Belle,* a 170-foot sternwheeler that featured many luxurious touches, to use in the passenger trade. Captain Humberstone had been running for a year on the Minnesota River, where he had staked out a townsite at South Bend, a few miles above Mankato. He intended to move his family to Minnesota and run his new boat out of St. Paul.

Winona, Minnesota, riverfront just four years after the first claim shanty was built here for Captain Orrin Smith. Front Street is filled with farmers' wagons loaded with grain to be shipped by steamboat. Photo c. 1856. Winona County Historical Society.

In May 1854 the *Belle* started from St. Louis, packed with immigrants (most of whom were intended for his new town) and loaded with freight. At St. Paul she was received with three hearty cheers. But the boat failed to get over the rapids at Carver and the captain, it was said, abandoned "the river, townsite and all," in disgust and went back to St. Louis. Other, smaller boats could navigate the Minnesota River, however, and soon its banks were dotted with speculative towns.

St. Paul Is the Goal of Fleeing Slaves

Not many people today realize that during the early 1850s St. Paul was a way station on the Underground Railway, the escape route of the fugitive slave. At the time St. Paul had a free black population of 30 or 40. Minnesota had been created as a free territory but federal law protected visiting slave owners who brought their slaves with them. Newspapers promoted the healthful climate to vacationing southerners, and many did travel north on the Mississippi with their slaves to stay at hotels in St. Paul. If any slaves escaped, they were supposed to be returned to their masters, and the sheriff was called out to find the runaways.

But St. Paul and other upper river towns had organizations of antislavery activists in place who could quietly spirit the fugitive to freedom. And in fact, according to Joseph Farr, a black man who came to St. Paul in 1850 as cabin boy on the *Dr. Franklin,* the activists secretly made arrangements to assist slaves in getting away from their owners. In Galena, said Farr, slaves were disguised and stowed with the freight on the *Franklin;* the boat would be met at the levee in St. Paul where the fugitive was taken off and hidden until safe from pursuit. Some stayed in Minnesota's free black communities, while others continued on to Canada.

Southern steamboats often rented crews of slaves from planters, but few of these boats plied the Mississippi above St. Louis for fear of liability if their black crew members walked off (for they were in no way restrained). In southern ports

Lodging in St. Paul in 1849

Every thing here appeared to be on the high-pressure principle. A dwelling house for a family could not be rented. The only hotel was small and full to overflowing. Several boarding houses were thronged. Many families were living in shanties made of rough boards fastened to posts driven into the ground, such as two men could construct in one day. It was said that about eighty men lodged in a barn belonging to [Henry] Rices' new hotel, which was not yet completed. Two families occupied tents. . . . I tarried a day or two at a boarding house, consisting of one room, about 16 feet square, in which sixteen persons, men, women and children, contrived to lodge.

E. S. Seymour, *Sketches of Minnesota, The New England of the West*, 1850

they could be sure the human property would be returned, but in northern cities there was every chance they would not be. In any case, a slave worth possibly $1,000 was too valuable to risk on the deck of a riverboat where he might be injured or drowned, as the courts usually allowed the slave owner to recover damages from the steamboat owners.

So This Is Going West!

The event that really opened the floodgates of immigration into the Upper Mississippi was the coming of the railroad, at first to Rock Island, then in quick succession to Galena, Dunleith, Fulton and La Crosse. Passenger traffic became so thick on Upper Mississippi steamboats that travelers who were able to get a stateroom were considered lucky. The rest had to sleep on the cabin floor or travel as deckers. Incoming trains

The 330-ton sidewheeler **Northern Belle**, built for the Minnesota Packet Company to meet the trains at Dunleith and La Crosse, was added to the line in 1856 with Preston Lodwick as master. This photo was taken at the Wabasha, Minnesota, levee. Photo Winona County Historical Society.

were met by runners for the different boats, who pounced upon the startled immigrants and travelers and hustled them aboard their steamer.

According to one passenger headed for St. Paul with 500 others on Preston Lodwick's *Northern Belle*, "Staterooms were entirely out of the question, and bunks upon the floor or seats at the table were at a premium. Standing at the lower end of the cabin and gazing upon the hundreds of persons whose beds covered almost every foot of the cabin floor, I intuitively exclaimed, `This is going West!'"

CHAPTER TEN

People on a Riverboat

Besides the officers, the crew of a riverboat included cabin staff and the deck crew. While all boats had a captain who was the officer in command, on smaller boats officers might do double duty and on the largest there might be second and third grade officers as backup. Crews ranged in size from four or five deckhands, sufficient to operate the smallest vessels, to the 121-person crew carried by the 1,117-ton *Eclipse* in 1852.

According to data gathered by the government, the average western steamboat in 1843 measured 154 tons and carried a crew of 21. The larger boats might have a deck crew of 50, but these were not often seen on the Upper Mississippi until the 1850s.

The Officers

The officers responsible for the management of the boat were the captain, clerk and mate. These officers represented the interests of the owners, and, indeed, often were the owners or part owners of the riverboat. The managing officers did not need to be skilled in the operation of the boat, but the engineers and pilots did need professional qualifications. In practice, on the Upper Mississippi many of the captains had "reached the roof" from the pilot house, and many a man who started out as clerk got his own

boat eventually. On smaller steamboats on the upper river, the captain was also the pilot and mate, and probably did the clerk's business as well.

Officers' accommodations were similar to those of the passengers. The captain usually had private quarters and on boats large enough to have a texas deck, the captain always occupied the forward cabin with the mate and other officers ranged in staterooms behind him. The captain and clerk joined the passengers at meals

---

Monthly Rates of Pay in the 1850s

Captain, $300 (about $6,500 today)
Pilot, $500   (about $10,800 today)
Chief clerk, $200
Mud clerk, $100
Mate, $150
Chief engineer, $200
Second engineer, $150
Steward, $200
Cooks, waiters, maids, bartenders, $50
Deckhands and Firemen $50
Watchman, $50 (about $1,000 today)
Ship's carpenter, $150

Walter Heyler, *Steamboat Traffic on the Upper Mississippi River 1850-1860*, 1919

in the main cabin; other officers ate at a second table or in the messroom.

Most officers were paid by the month, but pilots were usually hired for the trip, as they worked only the stretch of river they knew. The captain, and sometimes the clerk and mate, were paid by the year. The highest paid officers were generally the pilots—the most skilled and hence most in demand—with the captain next, and the chief clerk and chief engineer about even.

The Captain

The foremost officer on a riverboat was the captain, also known as the "old man." The captain answered only to the owners, and as the captain was generally sole or part owner of the boat he commanded, in general he answered to no one. However, it was a part of river etiquette for the captain not to interfere with the duties of the other officers, especially of the pilots. Generally the captain left the running of the steamboat to his mate and the pilots, being more concerned with managing the boat as a business enterprise. He decided questions of policy, and took charge directly only in case of accident or other emergency.

In the early days of steamboating, captains may have had little expertise in running a boat, some even becoming captain through purchase of a steamer. Others came to the trade through experience on keelboats and flatboats. But by the 1840s most captains had become skilled in handling the boat and machinery.

Because the captain was so closely identified with his boat, he needed to be able to impress

> ## Long Live the War Eagle and Captain Harris
>
> We were witness on Saturday last to a scene on the Levee at Galena that is worthy a notice in this age of selfishness. A poor woman, with a family of five children, sat crying amid the noise and bustle of that place, when Capt. [Smith] Harris, of the War Eagle, meeting her, inquired the cause. Finding she came from Pittsburgh on some packet; and had lost her husband on the trip of cholera . . .[he] ordered her to be put on board his boat, as she was destined for St. Paul, and made comfortable. After the War Eagle had left Dubuque, at the solicitation of Capt. H., a subscription was taken up among the passengers, and $25.60 raised for her, the Captain giving the lady with her children a free passage and devoting every attention to the wants of herself and children.
>
> *Minnesota Democrat* (St. Paul) May 1, 1854

people with his own abilities and to have a style or reputation that would attract passengers. The captain generally did all the hiring and firing, and therefore had to be a good judge of human nature. Because he was financially responsible for the boat and cargo, it was his decision whether the steamer would stop or go on, respond to a hail or pass the opportunity, chance Lake Pepin with the ice forming or turn back. Just as with ships at sea, the river code of honor required the captain to be the last to leave his sinking boat.

Daniel Smith Harris (1808-1893) was eldest of a family that came to Galena in 1823 to make their fortune in the lead mines. Smith Harris started on the river as cabin boy in 1829. In 1832, seeing the need for better transportation, he and brother Robert Scribe Harris built their own steamboat, the 26-ton **Jo Daviess,** possibly the first steamer built on the upper river. Smith Harris went on to buy, build, pilot and command 22 more, earning a reputation as a bold and aggressive commander. In 1848 he got up a competition against the Galena & Minnesota Packet Company with his fast boat **Senator,** which resulted in his being taken into the company. Crushed by the loss when his $63,000 **Grey Eagle** (worth $3 million today) hit the Rock Island railroad bridge and sank, Smith Harris retired from the river in 1861. His brothers Scribe, Martin Keeler, James Meeker and Jackson Harris all became steamboat engineers, pilots and captains as well, and operated a boat store in Galena. Photo State Historical Society of Wisconsin.

Agoston Haraszthy (1812-1869), university educated scion of a prominent Hungarian family, came to America in 1840 to make his fortune. Settling on the Wisconsin River, he founded the town of Sauk City, where he opened a store, mill, brickyard and grain and sheep farm. He also planted Wisconsin's first vineyards. In July of 1841 he purchased an interest in the steamboat **Rock River,** which he ran for several years on the Wisconsin and Mississippi rivers, providing the upper river's first scheduled packet service. In 1849 he led a wagon train to California, becoming in turn sheriff of San Diego County, city marshall, assayer of the San Francisco Mint and president of the California Agricultural Society. He is known as the father of the California wine industry, having introduced the Zinfandel grape and planted the Buena Vista vineyards at Sonoma. Still fascinated with steam power, in 1861 he launched a steamboat line in San Francisco Bay. After the Civil War he moved to Nicaragua, where he died in 1869. Photo San Diego Historical Society.

The Mate

Directly under captain in overall responsibility for the boat was the mate. He stood alternate watches with the captain, and acted as chief officer in emergencies. But the mate's main work was bossing the deck crew in handling and stowing cargo and fuel. He needed brawn to supervise the rough deckhands and skill to distribute cargo on the deck and in the hold so as to keep the boat in trim. Steamboats were always loaded with the most weight at the stern so that if the boat ran upon a sandbank it could generally be backed off. Every time cargo was unloaded, or additional cargo was added, the steamer needed to be rebalanced. A mate who knew what he was doing could give the steamer easy running qualities and keep pitching and rolling to a minimum.

The mate, however, took little part in the actual physical handling of the steamboat, except when supervising some repair or in charge of "grasshoppering," the process of jacking and winching the boat off a sandbar.

The Clerk

The reputation of a passenger boat depended a great deal upon its officers, and a boat's clerk was known and respected in communities up and down the river. The clerk, or chief clerk if there were more than one, was the steamer's financial officer. He was in charge of the business office, and usually had a cabin adjoining the main salon. It was his job to collect fares, assign staterooms, answer passengers' questions, issue tickets and freight bills, and see that everything

Russell Blakeley (1815-1901) was a Galena lead miner in 1839, starting on the river as a clerk in the 1840s. He was clerk on the first regular packet to St. Paul, M. W. Lodwick's **Argo,** in 1847, and one of the original owners of the Galena & Minnesota Packet Company. Blakeley served as clerk on the **Dr. Franklin** for several years, becoming her master in 1852 and later taking over the popular **Nominee** and the **Galena.** He retired to St. Paul in 1862 as a partner in a commission and forwarding firm, also taking an interest in several railroads and helping open the first steamboat line on the Red River of the north. Photo Minnesota Historical Society.

that came onto or left the boat was accounted for. The clerk kept the freight books that listed all consignments by weight, rate, shipper and destination and made out the bills of lading. It was also his responsibility to supervise loading and unloading and to be sure goods were left at the right place.

In the first clerk's absence the second clerk performed these duties, and it was usually the second clerk, or "mud" clerk as he was known, who had to stand out on the levee in all weather to supervise delivery and receipt of the freight.

George Merrick, an old-time riverman, claimed that there were two classes of officers above decks: the captain and chief clerk were the first class; the mate and second clerk were definitely the other. The second clerk not only stood the midnight watch and out in the mud, he also had to write up the delivery book in time for the next landing and was usually the officer who was sent ashore with wooding parties to be sure the number of cords paid for was actually taken aboard. However, many a clerk served his apprenticeship and moved up to command his own steamboat.

The Engineer

Most riverboats carried two engineers. Sidewheelers had independent engines for each paddlewheel, which might be called upon to run at any speed forward or reverse, and so each engine required its own operator. Each engineer stood a watch and would have his helper or "cub" to take the second engine on his watch. It was the cub who drew the onerous duty of scaling the boilers or cleaning out the mud drum after every run.

Sternwheelers, even those with two engines, had central controls that could sometimes be handled by one engineer, with help from a fireman at landings or in tight river bends. But the larger sternwheelers also carried two engineers: the first engineer, hired for his experience, was responsible for keeping the engines and boilers in good repair, while the second engineer, who was paid less, would stand his watch, handle his engine and keep an eye on the water level in the boiler. There his responsibility ended.

Some pilots seemed to believe that some second engineers were more agreeable to

The Engineer's Responsibility

The pilot at the wheel, directly over the boilers, is in blissful ignorance of the vital question agitating the engineer. He may at times have his suspicions, as the escape pipes talk in a language which tells something of the conditions existing below decks; but if the paddle wheels are turning over with speed, he seldom worries over the possibilities which lie beneath him. His answer to the question, whether the water is below the safety point, comes as he feels the deck lifting beneath his feet, and he sails away to leeward amid the debris of a wrecked steamboat.

George B. Merrick, *Old Times on the Upper Mississippi*, 1909

Steamboat pilot in the pilothouse. The pilot usually stood to one side or the other of the immense pilotwheel. He communicated with the engine room by a speaking tube and a system of bells. In poor visibility, the globular nighthawk mounted ahead of him on the jackstaff enabled him to find the horizon. Engraving from *Scribners Monthly*, 1874.

narrowing the boat's safety margin by carrying lower water and hotter steam in order to make faster time. On the whole, western riverboat engineers were poorly trained and often ignorant of the limits of their equipment. Pilots and owners with a timetable to meet often favored the "hot engineer" who drove the machinery with little concern for the risk.

The Pilot

The highest paid officer on a riverboat was invariably the pilot, or pilots—as most steamboats ran at night as well as by day and therefore needed two. The pilot was responsible for the course of the boat. That meant he needed a knowledge of the river that allowed him to steer around sandbars, snags and sunken wrecks, to know where the currents were strongest and the water deepest, and what the effect of the wind would be on the superstructure.

The safety of the boat depended on how well the pilot could read his stretch of river. He had only natural landmarks to guide him, no channel markers or shore lights. From the pilothouse at the highest point of the boat, sometimes fifty feet above the river, the pilot was connected to the engine room by a series of bells and often a speaking tube. With the bells he could instantly ask the engine room for full or half speed; to stop, back, or come ahead; or to change

What Sort of Men Steamboat Pilots Are

In the first place, they do not allow anyone to dictate or give them any advice when on duty, not even their pardners. If their pardner should say "If you run this way or that way, you will run aground" they would reply: "It is my watch now; when you come on watch you can run wherever you please." I have known pilots that would run a boat into jeopardy before they would condescend to take advice from their pardners. If there was a very bad dark night for a boat to run, and you should be called up to go on watch, and you should say, "This is a very bad night, or a very black night," your pardner would reply, "Oh, no, it is a very fair night to run," and at the same time it was a much as he could do to keep the boat in the river.

Then again, if a parcel of pilots met together on shore, who had just come up the river when it was a bad stage of water for boats to run, they would commence talking about certain places where there was shoal water, and one would say: "How did you run at such a place? As I came up I did not find much water. " And the other pilot would answer: "Oh, I came along there in the night and I had no trouble, found plenty of water." And at the same time he had probably butted the sand bar half the night, trying to get over.

On one occasion . . . it was 12 o'clock at night and the fog was raising and getting thick. I said to my pardner, "You will have to lie by tonight." "What for?" he replied. I told him the fog would stop us and he answered, "Oh I never lay a boat by: I run her until she lays herself by." So in a short time, he ran her hard and fast aground and it took the balance of the night to get her off.

So in a general way pilots are men, very consequential and self-conceited in their way; they think they know it all—which they cannot deny and tell the truth. I say this with all due respect to them as I have been a pilot for nearly fifty years myself.

John Scott Elder, old-time pilot, quoted in Frederick Way, Jr., *Way's Directory of Western River Packets,* 1950 ed.

direction on either engine.

A cub pilot might be steersman on easy stretches of the river, but the pilot always supervised and rarely left the wheelhouse. Special pilots were put on to navigate the boat over rapids where inches might make the difference. In low water, two men were often at the wheel, as control of the boat might depend on carrying full steam ahead.

Carpenter and Blacksmith

Few steamboats made a trip of any length without the need for some type of repair. On the Upper Mississippi the chief danger was from snags and floating debris that could take out several buckets on the paddlewheel or punch a hole through the boat's hull. The ship's carpenter stood ready to repair all these wood parts, replace guards brushed off by brush, or fashion whatever crates and boxes were required. James Ward of St. Louis, later master on *Saint Peters, Excelsior* and *York State* and president of the Northern Packet Line, started as the carpenter on *Ione.*

Boilers, flues and engines were made of iron before steel became readily available and many boats carried a blacksmith who could make on-the-spot repairs. When smokestacks got shortened by overhanging tree branches, it was the smith who fashioned new ones from the pieces so the smoke would clear the pilot house. Most engineers—with the help of a fireman or two—could do the work of a blacksmith, and were able to keep the boat supplied with bolts, clamps and chimney guys.

The Cabin Staff

On big passenger steamers, cabin crews included stewards, cooks, chambermaids, cabin or pantry boys and waiters. On smaller boats, the cook might be the entire staff. Passenger boats competed on the expertise and efficiency of their cabin staff and on the fine table they set. On these boats, the cabin staff were recruited from the best hotels, and the service they gave was comparable. The first cook and first steward received wages similar to officers of lower ranks (that is, the second engineer and second mate), but the wages paid the rest were even less than the deck crew got.

Cabin boys and waiters slept on the floor of the cabin along with servants of the cabin passengers, but they at least shared with the cabin pas-

Stephen B. Hanks (1821-1917), a cousin of Abraham Lincoln, started on the river in 1842 piloting floating log rafts. In 1846 he switched to piloting steamboats between Galena and St. Paul, first on **Amulet** and later on Smith Harris's **Dr. Franklin No. 2.** In 1850 he was first to take a steamboat, the **Anthony Wayne,** to the foot of St. Anthony Falls. He was pilot on **Galena** when she raced **War Eagle** through Lake Pepin and beat her to St. Paul in 1857 and when she burned and sank at Red Wing MN in 1858. He later served as master of several packets and raftboats, finally retiring in 1892 at the age of 70. Photo Washington County Historical Society.

sengers the safest part of the boat. Most crews were mixed, that is they contained men, boys and some women, both African American and white. They were usually hired by the season. Sometimes hunters also were hired to rustle up game for the table.

Hail to the Kitchen Crew!

It was a saying of the river that if you wished to save the meals a passenger was entitled to on his trip, you took him through the kitchen the first thing when he came aboard. The inference was, that after seeing the food in course of preparation he would give it a wide berth when it came on the table. . . . Things must be done in a hurry when three meals a day are to be prepared and served to three or four hundred people; and all the work had to be accomplished in two kitchens, each ten by twenty-feet in area—one for meats and vegetables and the other for pastry and desserts.

George B. Merrick, *Old Times on the Upper Mississippi,* 1909

The Steward

The steward was responsible for providing for meals at stated times, cooked and served in a satisfactory manner. Under the steward on a bigger packet were one or two assistants, plus meat cooks, vegetable cooks, pastry cooks and breadmakers, assistant cooks and poultry "dressers," and a force of waiters and pantrymen. Generally on the smaller boats, geared to the freight trades, the fare was ordinary, or even poor. But the better passenger boats prided themselves on setting a good table, which was an attraction for the traveling public on a par with the boat's cabin decor and speed. On northern steamboats the steward usually had to deal with only two seatings for each meal: white passengers and officers first, then the servants, passengers' servants and black passengers at a second sitting.

Although passenger packets carried crates of poultry and even milk cows, few big steamers could carry enough fresh food to feed up to 300 cabin passengers for five days, and so shortages had to be corrected when the boat put in at a landing.

It was also the steward's job to gently awaken sleepers on the cabin floor so that tables might be set for breakfast. His assistant in charge of the waiters would have the cabin "put to rights," and the cabin steward or stewardess would supervise the chambermaids in making up berths. A good steward was sought by many steamboat owners, and his pay was often commensurate with that of the captain.

Musicians

In flush times all sorts of inducements were offered passengers to board a given steamboat. In addition to the boat's speed and elegance, and its fine foods and wines, many boats carried a band or cabin orchestra to provide "dinner" music. Often the musicians were free blacks who were hired as waiters, barbers and baggage handlers, and got to make a bit more by playing and singing and

Sam Marshall Was an Artist

One of the boats on which I served employed a sextet of negro firemen, whose duty, in addition to firing, was to sing to attract custom at the landings. . . .

The leader, Sam Marshall . . . was an artist. It was his part of the entertainment to stand on the capstan-head, with his chorus gathered about him, as the boat neared the landing. If at night, the torch fed with fatwood and resin threw a red glow upon his shining black face, as he lifted up his strong, melodious voice, and lined out his improvised songs, which recited the speed and elegance of this particular boat, the suavity and skill of its captain, the dexterity of its pilots, the manfulness of its mate, and the loveliness of Chloe, its black chambermaid. This latter reference always "brought down the house."

George B. Merrick, *Old Times on the Upper Mississippi,* 1909

passing the hat. Musicians also played for dances in the cabin and staged impromptu concerts on the guards to attract customers while the steamboat was in port. Some of these performers were so popular they became the boat's best advertisement.

Barbers

Gentlemen wearing fancy facial hair thought they required the services of a trained barber for their morning shave. Many of these dandies traveled with their own servants, of course, but it did a boat owner no harm to advertise the quality of the barbering available.

Barbers, who were usually free blacks, were recruited from the river towns where their services were also in demand, and were a part of the cabin crew.

Bar Owner and Bartenders

In the 1840s and '50s all the packets featured bars, and, it would seem, most of the men who worked and traveled on them drank. The barkeeper, sometimes called the "spiritual adviser," was usually the best source of news and rumor, and when a steamboat landed the bar was besieged by eager "boarders," anxious to get news from below.

On many boats the bartender owned the bar, renting the space in the forward cabin, and it was usually a profitable venture. In fact, the popular saying was that owning a bar on a steamboat was better than owning a gold mine. "Billy" Henderson, bar owner on the *Excelsior,* also had a fresh fruit business, selling oranges and lemons wholesale along the river.

Tending bar on a riverboat was not difficult work. While some travelers might want their cocktails and juleps, most took their whiskey straight. The temperance movement of the 1840s seems to have applied to very few steamboats. When Captain Orrin Smith removed the bar from his boat, the passengers who desired to drink fortified themselves with jugs. There were some "reformers," who not only banned the bar and served only ice cream and soda water, but prohibited smoking and card playing as well. However, very few captains were willing to forgo profit for principle.

The Deck Crew

More than half a boat's crew was the deck crew, consisting of unskilled laborers. A deck crew of twenty-five included about twenty deckhands (roustabouts or rousters) and four or five firemen (stokers). In the early years of steamboating, slaves were employed extensively on steamboats in the Lower Mississippi valley, and by 1850 were the principal labor for steamboats operating chiefly in slave territory. But above St. Louis they were rarely used because of the risk of escapes.

Free blacks were also employed on steamboats, but seldom as deckhands. The great majority of African Americans were found in the cabin crews. In general, the roustabouts were white, and, until the heavy immigration of the 1850s when Irish immigrants sought the jobs, most were native-born Americans.

Deck crews lived, worked, slept and ate on deck with the deck passengers. Their meals

Black flies and mosquitoes were only part of the deck hands' misery. All cargo had to be moved by hand, carried on the backs of the rousters over the narrow landing stage that was likely to move with the boat. Deck hands loading **America,** year unknown. Winona County Historical Society.

consisted of leftovers from the cabin, all piled together with plenty of boiled potatoes. Some larger boats might furnish bunks, and some even had a messroom that converted to a bunkroom, but this would have been thought a novelty on the Upper Mississippi.

Deckhands were men of all work on the steamer; they manned the winches and pumps and handled cargo, a backbreaking job when all cargo had to be brought in by carrying or pushing it over a narrow gangplank. Not until the late 1840s were there any mechanical derricks to aid in moving freight. Deckhands did not stand watches, but were on call any time of the day or night. In addition to sharing with deck passengers the part of the boat most vulnerable to accidents, deckhands were exposed to the hazards of working with the machinery, cargo and lines, and the constant danger of falling overboard while attending to duties.

Firemen got shorter shifts and, sometimes, slightly higher wages in recognition of the heavy, constant work they did. At all hours of the day and night they faced the steamboat's roaring fires on an open deck and were required to carry aboard the twenty-five to seventy-five cords of firewood needed each day, each man staggering up the narrow gangplank with six or eight 4-foot logs at a time. Sometimes (as during a race) the roustabouts and even deck passengers helped with wooding.

Freight Handling

Dirtier and more toilsome work than this landing of the freight I have seldom seen. Heavy boxes, barrels of flour and whiskey had to be lifted and rolled up steep paths in the soft sand to the summit of the bank. Often the paths were so narrow that but one man could get hold of the end of a barrel and lift it, while another hauled it from above, their feet sinking deep at every step. Imagine a gang of forty or fifty men engaged in landing boxes, casks, sacks of corn and salt, wagons, livestock, ploughs; hurrying, crowding, working in each other's way, sometimes slipping and falling, the lost barrel tumbling down upon those below; and the mate driving them with shouts and curses and kicks as if they were so many brutes.

John T. Trowbridge, *The Desolate South, 1865-1868* (1956)

All steamboat hands worked as casual laborers. They were hired at the levee for the trip and then put off at whatever port they found themselves when not needed. Most had no opportunity for real family life and lived in boarding houses when not engaged. The work was so hard a man might make two trips, then take time off to recover while he drank up his pay.

What Happened to the Boats?

Of the 255 upper river steamboats positively identified in the Appendix, more than half succumbed to the dangers of the river and few escaped some accident during their careers. Most river steamboats had very short lives, in any case, four years being the average during the 1823 to 1854 period, and it was not uncommon for a boat to be lost in its maiden year. Those that did not suffer a nonrepairable accident simply "wore out."

Sunken Trees, or Snags, Destroyed Many

By far the greatest danger to the Mississippi riverboat was from snags and floating debris. Fifty-one boats, which is 20 percent of the boats listed, were sunk after being snagged. A snag was formed when a tree fell into the river and became fixed in the riverbed, ready to impale any boat that ran on it. Most steamers that hit a snag went to the bottom in two to five minutes. A great many boats ran on snags or hit other wrecks during their careers, but were able to be put back into service.

Four of the boats listed here sank after collision, although many more were in collisions that left them repairable. And twenty-three of the boats were lost when they foundered, were stove on a rock, or sank from unnamed causes.

Steamers Only "A Pile of Kindling Wood"

The next largest cause of loss of upper river boats was fire. In our list, a startling thirty-three steamers burned, many in wharf fires that consumed several boats at once. On May 17, 1849, a disastrous fire at St. Louis destroyed twenty-three steamboats, among them *Alexander Hamilton, Boreas, General Brooke, Montauk, Red Wing* and *St. Peters.*

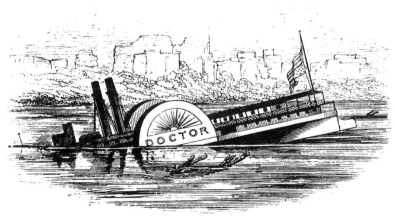

Wreck of the **Dr. Franklin,** lost in collision with the 296-ton **Galena** at McCartney, Wisconsin, in May 1854. It was sketched by Laurence Oliphant as he traveled from St. Paul to Galena a short time after the accident. The wreck remained until 1932 when a U.S. dredge removed it. From Oliphant, *Minnesota and the Far West*, 1855.

Fire was an ever-present danger in steamers that were lightly built of combustible painted wood: one writer describes a steamboat's super-structure as "little more than an orderly pile of kindling wood." Once started fires were nearly impossible to control. Any small fire—live coals on the deck, careless passengers, cinders falling from the smokestacks—could easily be fanned into an inferno. In addition, many boats carried readily combustible freight and used straw for packing—and all had stacks of dry firewood. Lifeboats were unknown, and few people could swim, so once a boat was ablaze the only hope of safety for passengers and crew lay in getting the boat ashore.

Another menace was ice, which crushed eleven of the boats listed and damaged many more. Six of them—*Bon Accord, Federal Arch, G.*

Twenty-three steamboats were destroyed when a fire got started on the St. Louis levee on May 17, 1849. Blazing boats got loose and careened downriver setting more boats on fire. Engraving by Scattergood in James T. Lloyd, *Lloyd's Steamboat Directory and Disasters on the Western Waters*, 1856.

W. Sparhawk, Highland Mary, Lamartine and *Shenandoah*—were lost in one huge ice gorge that smashed forty boats wintering at St. Louis in February of 1856. While the river at St. Louis did not freeze over, boats were not always safe there during the spring breakup when giant ice dams sometimes came crashing down the river.

Many other boats were damaged attempting to dodge drifting ice in Lake Pepin, only to be caught by a wind shift that sent them sweeping up onto the shore along with the ice. Eight of the boats in our list were stranded, which can mean blown onto shore in a windstorm or grounded midstream on a sandbar and left to the mercy of the wind and current.

Explosions Few, But Deadly

Boats on the upper river seemed to suffer fewer explosions than Mississippi riverboats in general. Apparently only two were lost through explosion, although at least six more suffered explosions or flue collapses that could be repaired. Passengers feared explosions the most, and with reason. Accidentally blowing up a boiler, beside killing those on deck in the path of the blast and hurtling many others into the water, would stop the boat's engines, leaving it adrift and burning in the middle of the river. Fire might also cause secondary explosions as it reached volatile cargo such as gunpowder. In general, explosions, while fairly small in number, were responsible for at least half the lives lost in all

The Hot Engineer

Men with a reputation [as a hot and fast engineer] were sought and always had a position. . . . I don't think they ever took into consideration the tensile strength of the iron to know the pressure to the square inch or anything of that kind. The only thing was to make the boat go and to avoid breaking the machinery, very little concern about blowing up and hurling all to Kingdom come . . . hot engineers and close fit pilots were sought by all commanders of boats. . . . There was no such thing as a pilot's or engineer's license. In those good steamboat times a man stood upon his merits.

> Wilson Daniels, "Steamboating on the Ohio and Mississippi Before the Civil War," *Indiana Magazine of History* 11.

riverboat accidents.

These known losses account for only a little over half of the boats that visited the Upper Mississippi. For most of the rest there was no disastrous last adventure. Seventeen are known to have been dismantled or rebuilt with another name, but most simply disappear from the registration lists. Some were probably broken up and sold for scrap. Others were simply abandoned, even though they might be only a few years old, because they had already worn out or would cost too much to repair. Those beyond the ability of the ship's carpenter to fix were probably left to rot in a boatyard somewhere.

Collapse on the Franklin No. 2

This boat collapsed the outside flue of her starboard boiler, August 22d, 1852, on the Mississippi river, five miles above St. Genevieve. Thirty-two persons were killed, or so badly wounded that death in every case was the result. Every person on deck who happened to be aft of the engine at the time of the accident was scalded to death. None of the cabin passengers were injured.

> James T. Lloyd, *Lloyd's Steamboat Directory and Disasters on the Western Waters*, 1856.

Upper Mississippi Steamboats: 1823–1854

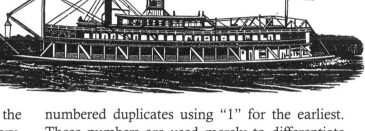

The 255 steamboats in this appendix are documented as having run on the Upper Mississippi above Galena, Illinois, during the period between the advent of the *Virginia* in 1823 and the end of 1854, the year of the Grand Excursion. Each boat has its own story. Most reached the St. Peters, the area centered on Fort Snelling at the mouth of the St. Peters (now Minnesota) River in the Minneapolis–St. Paul metro area. Some of these boats may have come only as far north as the Wisconsin River, La Crosse or Lake Pepin. However, boats that operated only below Galena have been omitted.

It is likely this list can be expanded, as there were at least seventy-five more steamers operating south from Galena during the period. About half of these can be found at St. Paul after 1854, but not earlier.

Information Included

The following information is included for each steamboat when known: rig (sternwheel or sidewheel), gross tonnage (rounded to whole number), year and place of construction, size, equipment (engines, boilers, etc.), year of appearance on the Upper Mississippi and final disposition. Because there are many cases of boats carrying the same name, the authors have numbered duplicates using "1" for the earliest. These numbers are used merely to differentiate boats in this book; they may be different on other steamboat rosters. If a number is officially part of the steamboat's name it is written out as, for example, "No. 2." A question mark indicates missing or conflicting data. For brevity, abbreviations and sentence fragments have been used throughout, but should pose no problem for understanding. In many cases where cash values are noted, the equivalent in today's (2002) dollars follows in parentheses.

Among the boats described are several that spent much of their careers on other rivers. Riverboat captains habitually moved south as cold weather set in and often ran their boats on the Missouri and Ohio rivers while those rivers remained ice-free, moving to the Lower Mississippi and its tributaries during the winter. Others made one or two dashes to the Upper Mississippi, but never returned. Details of their service other than on the Upper Mississippi and after the 1850s have generally been omitted.

Sources for Steamboats

The names and tales of these steamboats were garnered from many places. The primary sources for statistics and histories of Mississippi steamboats are William M. Lytle and Forrest R. Holdcamper's *Merchant Steam Vessels of the United States 1790-1868* (known as the Lytle-Holdcamper List) and Frederick Way's *Packet Directory, 1848-1994*. Lists of Upper Mississippi steamboats and their captains were compiled by William J. Petersen, George Byron Merrick, Edward W. Durant, and Russell Blakeley. There are scores of books and articles dealing with Mississippi River steamboating, many of which are given in our Bibliography.

In addition, there are hundreds of traveler's accounts, settler's diaries, business records, bills of lading and pieces of correspondence that mention steamboat arrivals at various river towns and often confirm their cargoes. From 1915 through 1926, G. B. Merrick edited a column of many old-timers' reminiscent accounts and lists of steamboats in the Burlington *Saturday Evening Post*. Newspapers from river towns are a great source of detail, as they carried steamboat advertisements and often a summary of the boats in port and their destinations. Some U. S. government enrolments and harbormaster reports can be found with first-hand information on tonnage, rig, builders and ownership.

Many museums and historical societies have steamboat collections. A great deal of help was given this project by the collections of the Putnam Museum in Davenport, the Public Library of Cincinnati and Hamilton County in Cincinnati, the Mississippi River Museum in Dubuque, the Jo Daviess County Historical Society and the Galena Historical Museum in Galena, the Murphy Library at the University of Wisconsin–La Crosse, the St. Louis Mercantile Library at the University of Missouri–St. Louis, the Missouri Historical Society at St. Louis, the Western Historical Manuscript Collections at the University of Missouri–Columbia and the collections of the Minnesota Historical Society at St. Paul, the State Historical Society of Missouri at Columbia and the State Historical Society of Wisconsin at Madison. Many smaller collections also provided valuable local information. For complete sources, please see the Bibliography.

This record of pre-1855 steamboats is offered in the spirit of Jean Henry Fabré (quoted in Frederick Way's *Packet Directory*):

"If we had to wait until we knew every detail of the question studied, no one would venture to write the little that he knows. From time to time, a few new truths are revealed. . . . Others will come, who, also gathering a few fragments, will assemble the whole into a picture ever growing larger and ever notched by the unknown."

A

Admiral *1853–1862, sidewheel 245 tons.* Built at McKeesport PA: 169x26', engines 20"x5½', 3 boilers. Her first master was J. T. Stockdale of Pittsburgh. Capt. John Brooks had her at Stillwater and St. Paul several times in 1854, once bringing the bell for the 2nd Presbyterian Church. Said to be one of the finest packets and the safest and fastest boat on the river, her amenities included a bathroom with piped in hot and cold water. Brooks and others bought her and took her to the Missouri R. She was sunk and raised October 1858. Burned at Columbus KY Apr. 5, 1862.

Adventure *1835–1838, sternwheel 49 tons.* Built at Pittsburgh. In August of her maiden year she took survivors off the *Dubuque* (1), which had exploded, and towed the wreck to port. Capt. James Lafferty had her at Galena in 1836; Capt. Van Houten took over 1836–7. When she was only a year old a passenger described her as "a very small dilapidated and filthy boat." In August 1837 Fort Snelling commander, Maj. Plympton, was on board returning to post with his family. The *Adventure* was advertised for sale at the St. Louis wharf by Capt. Ball in February 1838 "in good order for spring business." Off registration lists 1838.

Agnes *1840–1846, sidewheel 85 tons.* Built at Pittsburgh. Operating from her first port, Pittsburgh, she was stove on the Rock Island rapids September 1840 en route to Prairie du Chien, incurring $8,000 ($166,000 equivalent) damage to boat and cargo. By 1841 she was in the St. Peters trade, Capts. B. F. Wood and Crawford, carrying Indian trade goods. Noted at the St. Peters 1845. Off the packet lists 1846.

Alexander Hamilton *1847–1849, sidewheel 212 tons.* Built at Cincinnati for the Galena–St. Paul trade and Capt. W. H. Hooper, she was advertised in St. Louis for Galena and Dubuque in 1848 and also visited Stillwater that July (Capt. J. Samuel Hooper) with goods for Rev. W. T. Boutwell and others. She later ran on the Missouri. Burned in the May 1849 wharf fire at St. Louis, a $15,000 (over $350,000 equivalent) loss.

Alhambra *1854–1863, sternwheel 187 tons.* Built at McKeesport PA and in the St. Paul trade from the start, she was also at Stillwater September and November 1854, Capt. Kennedy Lodwick. By 1856 she was owned by the Galena, Dunleith & Minnesota Packet Co., Capt. W. H. Gabbert. She was known as a reasonably speedy boat and was often one of the last boats of the season at St. Paul. She was sunk in 12 feet of water in Lake Pepin September 1856 upward bound with a heavy cargo, which was a total loss. Raised and refitted, by 1860 she was a immigrant boat, described by a passenger as "old and bad at the best." Burned and lost in 1863.

Alice *1852–1858, sternwheel 72 tons.* Built in California PA: 116x21x3.2', one boiler. Her first master was Capt. W. E. Ferris, Pittsburgh, who ran this small sternwheeler briefly on the Muskingum R. She was at St. Paul and Stillwater in 1854 from Burlington, with William Tibbals as pilot, E. D. Smith captain. She appeared on the Missouri R. in 1856; no longer on lists by 1858.

Amaranth *1841–1846, sidewheel 220 tons.* Built at Sharpsburg PA: 147x25x5½'. Two model open-hold barges, 140x20x4', first of the type, were built to be towed alongside her, which enabled her to haul immense freights. Capt. G. W. Atchison commanded her in St. Louis–Galena–Prairie du Chien trade and on the St. Croix in 1842. That year she was stranded on the Mississippi, a $15,575 ($338,000 equivalent) loss. She was rebuilt by Atchison and in May 1843 left the Galena docks for St. Louis with one of the biggest freights ever: 13,000 pigs of lead weighing 455 tons. She also plied the upper river. An 1846 St. Louis newspaper notes, "Amaranth has gone to docks to be broken up."

Amulet *1844–1848, sternwheel 62 tons.* Built at West Wheeling OH. An odd-looking craft with open hull, built for low-water work, she was on the Illinois R. in fall 1845; at Galena from St. Louis in April 1846; at Stillwater the same month. *Amulet* was the first boat piloted by well-known riverman Stephen Hanks. Snagged and lost 1848.

Annie *size, rig and date unknown.* Built before April 1840, when she was advertised in Galena for a trip to St. Paul. She was noted on the St. Croix R. that summer. Not positively identified.

Anthony Wayne *1846–1851, sidewheel 164 tons.* Built at Wheeling VA, with hull by Dunlevy & McNaughton, engines by Hobbs & Taylor, and boasting a steam whistle. In the Galena–St. Louis trade, Capt. Charles C. Morrison, she became a regular Stillwater–St. Paul packet from 1847–50. In 1850 a purse of $250 was offered for the first boat to reach the Falls of St. Anthony—Capt. Dan Able collected with this rather large boat. The same year Able had her up the Minnesota R. as far as Carver with an excursion party, the first steamboat to ascend that river any distance. She was piloted then by Louis Pelon and Thomas J. Odell; at other times

Stephen Hanks piloted her. In 1851, during high water, she landed passengers at Stillwater's Minnesota House on Main Street, 200 yards inland. Snagged and lost near Independence MO Mar. 25, 1851.

Arabia *1853–1856, sidewheel 222 tons.* Built at Brownsville PA: 181x31x5.5', 3 boilers. Known as the "Great White Arabia," she was at Stillwater and St. Paul from St. Louis several times in 1854. She also plied the Missouri, was boarded at Lexington MO in May 1856 by a citizens' committee that confiscated 2 cannons and 100 rifles consigned to free soilers at Leavenworth KS. She was snagged and lost on the Missouri R. later that year. There were many salvage attempts as she was reported to be carrying a large cargo of whiskey. The wreck was found in 1988 in a Kansas cornfield half a mile from the present river channel. Her top was gone, but in her hold was merchandise destined for upriver stores: clothing, boots, china, pickles, hardware, tobacco, and much more. The Arabia Steamboat Museum opened in downtown Kansas City MO in 1990.

Argo 1 *1833–1841, sidewheel 84 tons.* Built at Jeffersonville IN at a cost of $3,850 ($82,000 equivalent), she first operated on the Ohio R., and may have been rebuilt at Madison IN in 1839 with expanded tonnage. She made at least one trip to Fort Snelling in April 1840. Lyford was her master when she was stranded and lost near Frankfort KY December 1841.

Argo 2 *1845–1847, sternwheel 41 tons.* Built at Louisville KY. One of the first regular packets in the Galena–St. Peters trade 1846-7, she was frequently at Stillwater with her keelboat carrying corn, cookstoves and mill supplies. In 1847 she was noted at Galena from St. Croix Falls with 100 passengers and was owned and commanded by Kennedy and M. W. Lodwick, with clerk Russell Blakeley. Her sinking near Winona MN in the fall of 1847 led the Lodwicks, Blakeley and others to form the Galena & Minnesota Packet Co. with her replacement, *Dr. Franklin.*

Ariel *1837–1840, sidewheel 95 tons.* 125x17½x4½′. Built at Pittsburgh by principals of the American Fur Co., her captain was part-owner Joseph Throckmorton. In 1838 she made regular St. Louis–Prairie du Chien–St. Peters runs with traders' stores, returning with furs and passengers. That year *Ariel* brought up the Dakota annuity goods and in September was the second known boat to enter Lake St. Croix. She made 5 trips to the St. Peters in 1839 under Capt. Lyon, once unloading 20 barrels of whiskey at Grey Cloud Island. In April 1840 she carried Maj. John Bliss to his post at Fort Snelling, and thereafter she disappears.

Asia *1850–1854, sidewheel 199 tons.* Built at Monongahela PA and billed as "a capital low-water boat," she made 12 trips St. Louis to St. Paul in 1853 under Capt. S. E. Porter and Capt. Smith. Towing 1 or 2 barges and carrying a freight "that would astonish," she was at Stillwater in April and August of that year. She also stopped at Quincy, Pontoosac, Dallas, Burlington, Muscatine, Davenport, Keithsburg, Albany, Savanna, Galena, Dubuque, Guttenberg, Clayton City, Prairie du Chien, Lansing, Wild Cat Bluffs (Brownsville), La Crosse, Hammond's Landing, Nelson's Landing and Prescott. Lost in the ice breakup at St. Louis Feb. 2, 1854.

Atlas *1844–1847, sidewheel 135 tons.* Built at Pittsburgh. This very light draft boat was advertised as a St. Louis–Galena packet in 1846, Capt. Robert Reilly, and was at the St. Peters that year. She generally towed a barge. The night of Sep. 14, 1846, she collided with *Otter* killing one passenger; the boats were not seriously damaged and in October she was at Stillwater with goods and grain from St. Louis. Snagged and lost March 1847 near Clarksville MO.

Audubon *1853–1858, sternwheel 191 tons.* 155x 29′6″x4′6″, 3 boilers. Her hull was built at Murraysville VA and the machinery added at Cincinnati. She was at St. Paul from St. Louis September 1854, Capt. Charles Morrison; at Stillwater that October; and stayed in the trade through 1855. Burned and lost at Galena December 1858.

B

Badger State *1852–1862, sternwheel 127 tons.* 140x28x3½′. Built at California PA and owned by Hempstead & McMaster and Thomas Gordon of Galena, her first master was Capt. Samuel Humberstone. She was a regular visitor at Stillwater with goods for Falls St. Croix 1852-3; was running St. Louis—Dubuque in 1854, Capt. Hawkins. Snagged and sunk in the Des Moines R. 1853, she was raised and sold to Capt. Lewis Swarmes. Her long career ended in December 1862 12 miles above St. Louis when she hit the wreck of *Altoona.*

Banner *1830–1838, sidewheel 84 tons.* Built at Ripley OH. *Banner* was noted at Dubuque from St. Louis in May 1836, Capt. Dickinson, and probably did not come above the lead mining region. Off registration lists in 1838.

Bellevue *dates, rig and tonnage unknown.* An American Fur Co. invoice from 1836 shows "Bell-view" carried Indian trade goods and supplies to the Mendota MN post that year. Along with the blankets, cloth, beads and broaches, tobacco, scalping knives and gunpowder were 3 frock coats, a basket of champagne, a plough and set of wagon harness.

Ben Campbell *1852–1860, sidewheel 287 tons.* Hull built at Shousetown PA and completed at Pittsburgh: 200x29½x5', 3 boilers, 26' wheels, 18½" cylinders, 6' stroke. Built for the Galena, Dubuque & Minnesota Packet Co. under supervision of Capt. M. W. Lodwick, she was in the St. Paul–Galena trade by June 1852 and was running St. Louis–St. Paul in 1853. A first-class passenger and freight packet, she had 50 large staterooms but made no pretence to fast running and was sold in 1853 because she proved too slow and too deep. Noted at Stillwater, Capt. Orrin Smith, 1852-3; at St. Paul in 1853 with 500 tons of freight, the largest cargo of season, much of it for the government. In 1854 she was a regular St. Louis–Galena mail packet, Capt. Mattison, and in June was advertised for a pleasure party to the Falls of St. Anthony, Capt. Dan Able. Burned August 1860 while laid up at Buffalo IA. Her equipment went into a stern-wheeler of the same name.

Ben Franklin *Not positively identified.* There may have been more than one boat of this name that came to Minnesota—at least 13 steamboats have carried a version of the name. According to Thomas Hughes, who calls her the *Benjamin Franklin No. 1,* she was built at Brownsville PA in 1847. By 1849 she was an upper Mississippi boat, carrying stores destined for the Wisconsin pineries from Galena to the mouth of the Chippewa River on Lake Pepin and was on the St. Croix R., Capt. Louis Bourchereau. On July 20, 1851, Capt. M. W. Lodwick is said to have used her to carry a party of notables to Traverse des Sioux to witness the treaty signing. In 1853 *Ben Franklin* was chartered to take Minnesota Territory's exhibit for the New York Crystal Palace Exhibition from St. Paul to Galena. That exhibit was to include a live, wild buffalo that having finally arrived in New York City charged the directors and was summarily rejected as an exhibit. No *Ben Franklin* is listed in St. Paul arrivals for that year, and the name is likely confused with the *Dr. Franklin,* the boat usually commanded by M. W. Lodwick.

Ben West *1849–1853, sidewheel 241 tons.* Built at Brownsville PA: 170x26'6"x5'7", engines 17½"x6', 3 boilers. She usually ran in the Pittsburgh–St. Louis trade, Ambrose Reeder master, but was at Stillwater in 1853, and plied in the St. Louis–St. Paul trade in 1855. Fatally snagged on the Missouri R. in August 1855.

Berlin *1851–1857, sternwheel 54 tons.* Built in Oshkosh WI; one engine. First noted at St. Paul in 1852, she was described as "short, round, pot-bellied and slow running." In 1854 the government chartered her for the lumber inspection service. She was a regular on the Minnesota R. 1855–6, making 13 round trips in 1855. Dismantled 1857.

Bertrand *1844–1850, sidewheel 145 tons.* Built at Pittsburgh PA, she ran on the Upper Mississippi from her home port St. Louis, and was advertised by Capt. Charles H. Rogers for an excursion to the St. Peters in June 1846. Capt. John W. Keiser of Pierre Chouteau Jr. and Co. bought her in 1847 for use on the Missouri R. Lost at Bayou Sorrel LA in 1850.

Black Hawk *1852–1866, sidewheel 83 tons.* Built at Rock Island IL: 130x21', 30 staterooms. Capt. M. W. Lodwick had her built, then who sold her to the Galena & Minnesota Packet Co. for a low-water boat (she drew only 17"). She was at Still-water, Marine and Taylors Falls in 1852, and made 6 trips up the Minnesota R. that year under Capt. W. P. Hall. In 1853 she made 10 trips to St. Paul and Stillwater and kept up the schedule in 1854. During high water in 1853–4 she was a regular Minnesota R. packet, ferrying troops and supplies to Fort Ridgely. Although reported to have been one of the Grand Excursion boats, she cannot have been at Rock Island June 6, 1854, as St. Paul re-cords note her departing that day for Traverse des Sioux with the largest cargo of the season. She had various commanders including S. B. Harlow, R. M. Spencer and O. H. Maxwell. In 1858 she was purchased by Commodore W. F. Davidson for the Northwestern Union Packet Co.'s La Crosse–St. Paul run and last appeared in St. Paul in 1859. In 1862 the U.S. government chartered her for use as a hospital boat during the Civil War. Off lists 1866.

Black Rover *date, rig and tonnage unknown.* *Black Rover* was an early arrival at Fort Snelling, sometime before May 1826. She was among the boats chartered by the army to carry up public stores, Indian trade goods, military provisions and passengers.

Bon Accord *1846–1856, sidewheel 147 tons.* Built at St. Louis. An Upper Mississippi boat, she ran out of Galena for St. Paul under Capt. James L. Bipell in 1846; Capt. Hiram Bersie had her in the Galena–St. Peters trade in 1847, Galena–St. Louis 1848. In May 1849 she was at Galena with 64 cabin and 50 deck passengers, and was noted at St. Paul in October 1852. Lost in the ice breakup at St. Louis Feb. 26, 1856.

Boreas *1841–1849, sidewheel 157 tons.* She was built at Pittsburgh for Thomas M. Fithian and George Barnard who ran her in the St. Louis–Keokuk trade. Capt. Whitney had her at Stillwater in September 1845 with goods from St. Louis for Greeley, Blake & Brunell. She later ran on the Missouri R. Lost in the 1849 St. Louis wharf fire.

Brazil 1 *1838–1841, sidewheel 194 tons.* Built at Cincinnati: 160x23'. Capt. Orrin Smith bought her in 1838 "completely fitted up with staterooms, two berths in each, with doorways leading both into the cabin and out upon the deck." She was at Fort Snelling in June 1838, ran excursions to the St. Peters 1839 and 1840, appearing on the St. Croix in 1840. She struck a rock on the upper rapids in the spring of 1841 and sank, an $18,000 (today $367,000) loss, but was rebuilt as *Clarion*.

Brazil 2 *1842–1847, sidewheel 166 tons.* Built at Cincinnati: 144x22x5', 2 engines, 22' wheels, 30 staterooms. After *Brazil 1* was wrecked, Orrin Smith built this light-draft boat to operate from Galena. Renamed *New Brazil*, she was on the St. Croix R. in 1842 and was at the St. Peters in June 1843 again named *Brazil*. Off registration lists 1847.

Bridgewater *1842 – 1849, sternwheel 58 tons.* Built at Pittsburgh, she was one of the first packets to have her hurricane roof extended clear forward ward with the stacks cased in. She started on the Ohio, hit a rock in 1845, but was back in service at

Galena in 1846. She arrived at Stillwater the same year, Capt. R. M. Spencer, clerk E. H. Gleim. Removed from lists 1849.

Brunette *1852-1859, sidewheel 228 tons.* Built at Jeffersonville IN: 195x28.5x5.5′. She was designed to operate on the Missouri R. but was running on the Mississippi in 1853. Described as "a very pretty boat, neat but not gaudy," she advertised a ladies' cabin with 10 staterooms and main cabin with 42. Said one editor, "the saloon bar is a gem and the keeper thereof is a trump." She was noted leaving for St. Paul in June 1853, Capt. Willard; in 1854 she was in the St. Louis–Galena trade, generally towing barges. She also ran on the Illinois R. She was damaged in the ice break-up at St. Louis in 1856 and burned there October 1859.

Burlington *1837–1839, sternwheel 200 tons.* Built at Freedom or Monaca PA: 150x23½x6′, double rudder stern. Her owners were Joseph Throckmorton, Pierre Chouteau Jr. and Hempstead & Beebe of St. Louis. Capt. Throckmorton took her upriver for the first time in May 1837. In 1838 she was advertised for the Black, Chippewa, St. Croix and St. Peters rivers; by June she had made three trips to Fort Snelling to deliver 146 recruits and supplies for the Fifth Infantry. At various times she carried notables Col. John Bliss, George Catlin, Joseph N. Nicollet, John C. Fremont, Henry Atkinson, Franklin Steele and Elizabeth, widow of Alexander Hamilton, to the St. Peters. Off lists 1839.

C

Caleb Cope *1847–1856, sternwheel 79 tons.* Built at Glasgow PA. In January 1848 she was running on the Ohio, but by 1852 was owned by the Galena & St. Paul Packet Co. A small, fast boat, she was chartered for the St. Paul trade in early 1852 because the *Ben Campbell* was not ready. She was at Stillwater from Galena in May 1852 commanded by Capt. John Brooks, and returned again in 1854. She was one of the first boats engaged to tow log rafts through Lakes St. Croix and Pepin. Off records 1856.

Caledonia *1833–1838, sidewheel 122 tons.* Built at Ripley OH, she is listed on the Dubuque steamboat register as plying between that point and Prairie du Chien in 1837. Off the register in 1838.

Cavalier *1832–1838, sidewheel 98 tons.* Built at Ripley OH. She was one of the first boats to Galena in the early spring of 1836 and was a regular at Galena that year; she also hauled to Dubuque under Capt. Patterson. She was noted at Galena again in 1837, but may not have come higher than the lead region. Snagged and sunk with loss of two lives near Evansville IN in August 1838.

Cecilia *1841–1847, sternwheel 111 tons.* Built at Pittsburgh: 140x20′9″x4′5″. Joseph Throckmorton bought her and ran her in St. Peters trade in 1844. She was in regular service to Stillwater in 1844–6 commanded by Throckmorton, M. E. Gorman clerk. At the outbreak of the Mexican War in June 1846 she was pressed into service to haul troops from Forts Crawford and Armstorng to St. Louis. Off lists 1847.

Chippewa *1840–1843, sternwheel 107 tons.* Built at Pittsburgh for the American Fur Co., she was owned by Hercules Dousman and Joseph Throckmorton, who ran her on the Upper Mississippi.

Capt. W. P. Gorman commanded in 1840 and Capt. T. H. Griffiths in 1841–3 as she provided regular service to the St. Peters and the St. Croix R. Off lists 1843.

City Belle *1854–1863?, sidewheel 215 tons.* Built at Murraysville VA 1854 (possibly 1853). Capt. Kennedy Lodwick ran her regularly between Galena and St. Paul 1853?–6. She was at Winona with immigrants of the Minnesota Settlement Co. in May 1856 and was snagged and sunk that fall. Repaired, she was noted bringing horses, mules, cattle, sheep and hogs to St. Paul in 1857. A. T. Champlin commanded her part of 1858. She was a very short boat and said to be hard to steer. Apparently she migrated to the Missouri as a picture of her exists taken in 1863–5 at a Missouri R. landing. Reported burned at Red R. LA in 1862; final disposition unknown.

Clarion *1851–1860?, sternwheel 73 tons.* Built at Monongahela PA from the *Brazil* (1). In 1852 she towed a barge from Pittsburgh to Wheeling carrying that city's first locomotive. Next season she went to the St. Paul–Minnesota R. trade, which she plied under Capts. Samuel Humberstone and William Gabbert 1853–7. She had a "very big whistle in keeping with her name, so large that it made her topheavy." She was at Stillwater with her barge 1853–4; on the Minnesota R. 1853; made 23 trips to St. Paul in 1853, bringing down the first produce of the Minnesota Valley (1,200 board feet of black walnut from Babcock's mill). That fall she survived a boiler explosion that injured two. Capt. Sencerbox and Capt. O. D. Keep ran the indomitable *Clarion* in the Minnesota R. trade until she sank near the St. Paul levee about 1860.

Clermont No. 2 *1845–1851, sidewheel 121 tons.* Built at Cincinnati: 138x2′9″x4′5″. Named for the inventor of the river steamboat, *Clermont* started her career in Cincinnati. She was on the Missouri R. in 1846, then moved to the Mississippi; by 1848 she was running between Montrose and Rock Island. In 1849 she took a large pleasure party from Quincy to St. Paul and the Falls of St. Anthony. She sank on White R. AR with loss of 20 lives in December 1851.

Colonel Morgan *1853–1862, sternwheel 83 tons.* Built at Brownsville PA, her first home port was Pittsburgh, but this small sternwheeler was soon running on the Upper Mississippi. Capt. Reeves C. Jones had her on the Des Moines in early 1854, but she dropped out from the "total drying up" of that river. She was noted arriving at Stillwater in November 1854 "loaded to the guards," and also in 1855, and was a regular at St. Paul 1855–8. She was on the Missouri R. in 1856, Capt. William N. Hicks. No longer registered by 1862.

Confidence *1845–1849, sidewheel 139 tons.* Built at Wheeling VA. She was a big low-water packet (drawing just 10″ light) owned by Hannibal merchants and running St. Louis-Galena 1845–7, Alex Gordon, master. In 1847 she was in collision below Hamburg IL and sank, losing a cargo of groceries. She was raised and in May 1848 was advertised in St. Louis as a regular packet to Galena, Prairie du Chien, St. Peters and the St. Croix, Capt. Lusk. She was running on the Ohio R. Louisville-St. Louis in 1849 when she collided with the 257-ton *Brooklyn* and sank near the Kentucky shore.

Cora *1846–1853?, sidewheel 144 tons.* 139'8"x23' x4'9", single engine with stiff shaft, 18" cylinder, 5' stroke, two boilers. Her hull was built at Rock Island IL by Joseph Throckmorton, who had the machinery installed at St. Louis, and took command of her in 1846. She was a regular Stillwater packet 1846-9 (J. E. Gorman master 1849), first arrival at Fort Snelling in 1847, ran Galena to St. Peters in 1848 (R. A. Reilly master) and also made trips to St. Croix Falls. Sold in the fall of 1848 to Reilly for the Missouri R., she was snagged and sunk at Council Bluffs IA with loss of 15 lives in May 1851. She was apparently raised, as *Cora* was again reported at Stillwater in May 1853. Final disposition is unknown.

D

Daniel Hillman *1846–1855, sternwheel 145 tons.* Built at Smithland KY. *Dan Hillman* was at St. Louis in 1847, in the Galena trade for some time and also on the Illinois and Missouri rivers. In 1854 she was purchased by Capt. `Obe' Eames and taken to Stillwater to enter the rafting business, the first boat on the St. Croix that season. She also towed rafts in Lake St. Croix in 1855, and then disappeared. One source says she was dismantled at Stillwater.

Danube *1847–1852, sidewheel 156 tons.* Built at Brownsville PA, she started on the Ohio and Monongahela rivers and made at least one trip from Rock Island to St. Paul, Capt. Bargin (probably Barger), in October 1851. She struck rocks, was stove and sunk at Port Byron IL in fall 1852.

Dayton *1835–1845, sidewheel 111 tons.* Built at Pittsburgh: 125'4"x17'9"x5'2". Generally an Ohio R. boat, she made an excursion from Louisville to the Falls of St. Anthony in 1840. She exploded on the gulf coast of Texas with loss of 10 lives in September 1845.

Des Moines *1838–1844, sternwheel 93 tons.* Built at Pittsburgh; her name is also spelled *Demoine*. In October 1839 she was hired to bring Indian annuity goods to Fort Snelling. She appeared at least once more at the St. Peters in the 1840s with freight from Galena (for which she charged 75¢ per 100 pounds—a 50 percent premium). She was rebuilt as a barge in 1844.

Die Vernon *1850–1858, sidewheel 445 tons.* Built at St. Louis: 255x31.1x5.8'. The crack boat of the St. Louis & Keokuk Packet line, built at cost of $49,000 ($1.1 million) to replace a former boat of same name, this "floating palace" with over 100 berths made several trips to the Falls of St. Anthony from St. Louis in 1851. Capt. Rufus Ford ran her St. Louis–St. Paul in the summer of 1852, competing with steamers of the Minnesota Packet Co. The fastest (and largest!) boat on the upper river, she was challenged by every other boat including the Minnesota Packet Co.'s speedy *West Newton* (Capt. Smith Harris) in July 1853. *Die Vernon* won that race, making a record run of 84 hours, counting all stops, from St. Louis to St. Paul, averaging 9½ mph upstream. She was named for Walter Scott's heroine, Diana Vernon, but always spelled "Die." Retired in 1858.

Dispatch *1846–1854, sternwheel 45 tons.* Built at Freedom PA. *Dispatch* started out in Pittsburgh, but soon moved to the St. Croix where Capt. Edward Grant (a.k.a. Edouard Le Grandeur) ran her 1850-1. The boat may have been owned by Gen. Sam

Harriman of Somerset WI who used her to haul flour from his Apple (WI) R. mills to Stillwater. Capt. C. J. Bradley had her later on the St. Croix R. Off records in 1854.

Dr. Franklin (Old Doctor) *1847–1854, sidewheel 149 tons.* Built in the Dunlevy & McNaughton yard at West Wheeling VA: 156x24x4'2". She boasted the first steam whistle on Upper Mississippi. *Dr. Franklin* was in the Ohio R. trade in July 1847 and was sold that fall to the Galena–St. Paul trade. With Capt. M. W. Lodwick, master, R. Blakeley, clerk, she became the first boat of the Galena & Minnesota Packet Co. and was a regular at Stillwater and St. Paul 1848–53. In 1848 she brought the Winnebago Indians to their Minnesota reservation and in 1851 carried Red Wing's Dakota band to the Treaty of Traverse des Sioux (she was popular with the Dakota who called her `Great Medicine'). In 1849 Lodwick had her up the Chippewa R. Blakeley was her master in 1852 when she made 29 trips to St. Paul. In 1853 Capt. Preston Lodwick brought a pleasure party to St. Paul and invited leading citizens to join the party aboard the boat for 2 hours of dancing. She was in collision in March 1849, greatly damaged by fire in March 1853, and finally lost in collision with the 296-ton *Galena* (3) at McCartney WI May 1854. The wreck was revealed in 1932 when a U.S. dredge doing channel work uncovered and removed it.

Dr. Franklin No. 2 *1847–1853, sidewheel 189 tons.* 173x26'6"x4'4". Built for the Ohio R. at Wheeling VA, she was bought by the Harris brothers of Galena who ran her in opposition to the *Dr. Franklin* as a regular Galena–Stillwater–St. Paul packet. In April 1849 she was the first boat up to St. Paul, carrying news of the creation of the Territory of Minnesota. In 1850 Capt. Smith Harris piloted her up the Chippewa R. carrying goods for Knapp & Wilson Lumber Co. Harris delighted in racing the `Old Doctor' port to port; in 1853 with pilot Stephen Hanks he outran *Nominee*, prize boat of Minnesota Packet Co. in a race from Reads Landing to Galena, setting a new St. Paul–Galena record of 22 hours. The *Dr. Franklin No. 2* collapsed a flue in August 1852 killing 32 deck hands and deck passengers. Burned at St. Louis July 1853.

Dubuque 1 *1835–1837, sidewheel 74 tons.* Built at Pittsburgh in 1835, she was first noted on the upper river at Galena in April 1836, Capt. Smoker. In 1837 the river opened early, and on March 28 Capt. Atchison brought *Dubuque* into Galena and then into Dubuque. She probably did not come higher. While she was bound up from St. Louis in August of 1837, the larboard (left-hand) boiler exploded with terrific force, throwing scalding water and steam over the deck and snuffing out 21 lives.

Dubuque 2 *1847–1855, sidewheel 168 tons.* Built at Elizabethtown PA: 162x26x5'. Owned by Edward H. Beebe and Le Grande Morehouse, she was a regular in the St. Louis–Galena–Dubuque trade. In 1848 she appeared on the St. Croix R. and was at Galena in 1849 loading for Fort Snelling, E. H. Beebe master. Ice was forming when she was noted "whistling up" to the Galena levee in November 1851 with two barges in tow and one of the heaviest cargoes of the season. She was sold in May 1853 to St. Louis as a barge tow, but was again advertised in spring 1854 as a St. Louis–Dubuque packet, John Wesley, master. Foundered and sank on the Missouri R. 1855.

E

Eclipse 1 *1823–1826, sidewheel 168 tons.* 103′2″x18′6″x7′3″, square stern. She was built in Beaver PA and enrolled at Louisville Christmas Day 1823; she later operated out of New Orleans, Scudder Hart, master and owner. St. Peters Indian agent Lawrence Taliaferro records her arrival at Fort Snelling with government supplies before May 1826. Snagged and lost in 1826.

Eclipse 2 *1854–1860, sternwheel 156 tons.* Built at California PA: 150x27x4′. Not positively identified. A boat of this name arrived for the first time at St. Paul in May 1854, and is probably the sternwheeler noted here, first registered at Pittsburgh. This boat later ran on the Alabama R. A sidewheel *Eclipse* of 216 tons was also running during 1853–60 and ended up in Texas.

Editor *1851–1854 sidewheel 247 tons.* Built at Brownsville PA: 174x27½x5½′. She was in the New Orleans–Cincinnati trade in 1851, then on the Illinois R. and came into the St. Louis–St. Paul trade in spring 1854, Capt. J. F. Smith and later Capt. Brady. She was at Stillwater April and May 1854. That June she was noted arriving at St. Louis from St. Paul with a $230,000 ($4.9 million) cargo that included 4 boxes of gold. Sold to a New Orleans firm in 1859, she burned at Algiers LA in 1861.

Eldora *date, rig and tonnage unknown.* Chartered in 1840 in St. Louis by 80 people proposing to explore the Upper Mississippi and St. Croix R. to find the spot for a settlement, she is said to have gone as far as J. R. Brown's trading post at the head of Lake St. Croix (site of Stillwater). There is no other record of the boat or where the group ended up. The name may be Eldorado.

Emilie *1840–1843, sidewheel 220 tons.* Built in Pittsburgh. One of the first sidewheelers with independent engines, she was owned by Pierre Chouteau Jr. & Co. and named for the wife of its president. Operating from St. Louis, *Emilie* was noted at the St. Peters in 1841, Capt. Joseph La Barge, and was also on the Missouri R. La Barge was pilot when she was snagged and lost on Emilie Bend in the Missouri R. in 1843.

Enterprise 1 *1824–1827, sidewheel 68 tons.* Built at Louisville KY, her first home port was New Orleans. She was chartered by the army and appeared at Fort Snelling before 1827 with government supplies. Not recorded after 1827.

Enterprise 2 *1830?–1833, sidewheel 111 tons.* Built at Shousetown PA. Some records indicate she was built in 1831, but she was at Fort Snelling in the summer of 1830 and returned in June 1832. She was often chartered by the army; in 1831–2, under Capt. James May, she took troops upriver from Jefferson Barracks to Rock Island and Prairie du Chien to quell Indian disturbances. Capt. May had her in an early packet cooperative in 1831 with Joseph Throckmorton's *Winnebago*. Snagged and lost on the Illinois R. 1833.

Enterprise 3 *1849–1852?, sternwheel 50 tons.* Built as a barge and converted to steam at Paducah KY. At least 28 steamers built before 1868 carried the name *Enterprise*, hands-down the most popular riverboat name. A boat of this name and size ran on the Wisconsin R. 1849–51 under Capt. William H. Gabbert. She was expected at St. Paul in

November 1850, but fearing the freeze-up discharged her cargo at Red Wing MN and "turned tail." In 1852 John Scott was master, running Rock Island–Galena–Dubuque–St. Paul. *Enterprise* (3) was also on the Missouri R. in 1850, and on the Minnesota R. in 1851-2; in the summer of 1852 she went as far as Little Rapids (Carver MN) carrying settlers. Her disposition is unknown.

Enterprise 4 *1853–1855, sidewheel 50 tons.* Built at Fulton OH: 70x25x3'6", transom stern. Registered as new in 1853, she may be *Enterprise* (3) rebuilt. A regular St. Croix R. packet through 1855, she was small enough to deliver goods directly to Marine and Taylors Falls, and was also useful on the Minnesota R. Her machinery went into the *New Saint Croix* in 1855.

Envoy *1832–1837, sidewheel 91 tons.* Built at Cincinnati. This small sidewheeler drew about 5' of water loaded, but still managed to ascend the Wisconsin R. in 1837 as far as Fort Winnebago (Portage) with government supplies under Capt. Mims. She is not noted as plying above that river, but is recorded at Dubuque in 1836. Off lists in 1837. (Further description p.74)

Excel *1851–1856, sternwheel 79 tons.* 150x27x5', 2 engines 12x55", 2 boilers. Built at McKeesport PA, she ran on the Ohio and Illinois rivers, then on the Mississippi from St. Louis as a tramp steamer. She was at Stillwater and St. Paul, E. Williams master, J. J. Plets clerk, in August 1854 with 1,192 bushels of corn. Snagged and lost March 1856 in Osage Chute, Missouri R., a $5,000 ($100,000) loss.

Excelsior *1849–1861, sidewheel 172 tons.* 182x28x5'. She was built at Brownsville PA for Capt. James Ward and others and ran regularly in the St. Louis–St. Paul trade through 1857; was also at Stillwater from 1851–4. She was noted for the antlered deer head on her prow. A well-known character, `Billy' Henderson, owned the bar on the boat and sold oranges and lemons wholesale along the river. She arrived at St. Paul in June 1851 with Commissioner Luke Lea and took him, along with Gov. Alexander Ramsey and traders and chiefs of the Sioux, to Traverse des Sioux for the treaty signing. Her cargo included 77 head of cattle for the Indians. She was at St. Paul again in 1854. One of the largest boats to reach St. Croix Falls (1851) she was also first boat up the St. Croix in 1856. A steam piano was introduced on her that year, but it proved too loud and was removed. Off lists 1861.

F

F. X. Aubrey *1853–1860, sternwheel 246 tons.* Built at Brownsville PA. She started on the Missouri, running St. Louis to St. Joseph under Capt. Ambrose Reeder. In June 1854 she was noted departing St. Louis for St. Paul. It was a summer of very low water and few through boats, and it is not likely she got all the way. She was damaged in the ice break-up at St. Louis in February 1856. Sold to Pittsburgh in 1860, where she was dismantled; her machinery was used on *Arago*.

Falcon *1843–1849, sidewheel 133 tons.* Built at Freedom PA. She was a regular St. Louis–Dubuque–Potosi packet in 1845, shipping from the Wisconsin lead mines, when she holed her hull on the upper rapids. From 1846–7 Capt. Le Grande Morehouse extended her run to St. Louis–Galena–St. Peters and also hauled freight and excursionists to Stillwater. She sank in heavy ice January 1849 bound from St. Louis to the Illinois R.

Far West *1834–1841, sidewheel 200 tons.* Built at New Franklin MO: 136'x20'x6'. Although she bears the same name as a famous Missouri R. mountain boat, this *Far West* was built 35 years earlier. She spent most of her days on the Lower Mississippi. Her only mention on the upper river is her arrival in Dubuque in May 1836. Off lists 1841.

Fayette *1837–1843, sidewheel 112 tons.* Built at Brownsville PA. *Fayette* was chartered in April 1839 at Davenport to transport sutler's stores to Fort Snelling and mill machinery to Marine Mills. Passengers included principals in the lumber mill, a millwright, blacksmith and Mrs. David Hone, who was to be the company's cook. Probably the fourth boat to go up the St. Croix R. She sank between Alton and St. Louis about 1843.

Federal Arch *1850–1856, sidewheel 195 tons.* Built at Brownsville PA. She generally worked as a tramp between Pittsburgh and St. Louis, but was in the Upper Mississippi trade in 1853 and was logged at Dubuque that May. She was being dismantled when ice smashed her at St. Louis, February 1856.

Fire Canoe *1854–1858, sidewheel 166 tons.* Built at Ironton OH, near Cincinnati. She entered the Upper Mississippi trade in fall 1854 under Capt. Baldwin and continued in the trade 1855–7 under Capt. Spencer. A light-draft steamer, she was described by a St. Paulite as "about the best boat of her class we have seen this way." She was on the Minnesota R. in 1858, then was sold to the Missouri R. where she was snagged and lost in November 1858.

Fleetwood *1850–1852, sidewheel 212 tons.* Built at Brownsville PA for John B. Hall, this short-lived packet arrived at St. Paul in June 1851 and made a second trip from St. Louis that September. Snagged and lost in early 1852 on the Wabash R. near Terre Haute IN.

Fortune *1845–1847, sidewheel 101 tons.* Built at Louisville KY. Capt. Pierce Atchison bought her for $6,000 ($140,000) in April 1845 at Cincinnati and ran her in the St. Louis–Galena trade 1845–7 with through trips at intervals to Fort Snelling with government goods. She was at Stillwater in October 1845 with supplies for Greeley & Blake. In 1846 she sank her keelboat, which was loaded with 1,800 pigs of lead, at the mouth of Fever R. She hit a rock on the upper rapids and sank near Keokuk in 1847.

Frontier *1836–1841, sidewheel 63 tons.* Built at Cincinnati. In May 1836 Smith Harris arrived at Fort Snelling in charge of his newest steamer, *Frontier.* That summer he set the first speed record from St. Louis to Galena with her: 3 days, 6 hours. She operated on the Wisconsin R. and was the first steamboat on Rock R.—Harris piloted her as far as Dixon's Ferry (Rockford IL) in 1836. Off records 1841.

Fulton *date, rig and tonnage unknown.* Indian agent Lawrence Taliaferro lists a boat of this name bringing supplies to Fort Snelling prior to May 26, 1826. She is also advertised for the St. Peters at Galena in 1827. Her name is probably *Missouri Fulton* (see *Missouri Fulton* [1]).

G

G. W. Sparhawk *1851–1856, sidewheel 243 tons.* Built at Wheeling VA. She came from the Ohio R. to the Upper Mississippi, Capt. Charles Barger, and visited Stillwater in 1853. In June 1854 she joined the Grand Excursion to St. Paul under Capt. Monroeville Greene, and was in the St. Paul trade in 1855. She was snagged and sunk at Nininger Bend MN in 1855, but was raised and refitted. Lost in ice at St. Louis February 1856.

Galena 1 *1829–1838, sidewheel 105 tons.* Built at Cincinnati: single engine. Capt. David G. Bates had her built and hired Smith and Scribe Harris to bring her to the Upper Mississippi. She was frequently at Galena and Bates had her at Fort Snelling in 1829. She was renamed *Hawkeye* in 1832 and was in the Galena–St. Louis trade until 1837. Off the lists 1838.

Galena 2 *1841–1847, sidewheel 135 tons.* Built at Pittsburgh. Capt. P. Connolly had her in the Galena–St. Peters trade. In 1842 her machinery broke while bringing 350 soldiers to Forts Crawford and Snelling; on the way back she blew a cylinder and had to be towed in; she was nearly wrecked in a storm on Lake Pepin in 1845. Surviving all, in 1846 she was again at Galena, Cephas Goll master and John Stephens clerk. No longer on the lists in 1847.

Galena 3 *1854–1858, sidewheel 296 tons.* Built at Madison IN: 219x29', 46 staterooms. Built for the Galena & Minnesota Packet Co., she was at Stillwater in May 1854, and later that year took part in the Grand Excursion with D. B. Morehouse, master. In 1855 Russell Blakeley took over, then Kennedy Lodwick in 1856 and W. H. Laugh-

ton in 1857. In 1856, she was noted leaving Dunleith with over 800 passengers, mostly immigrants bound for Minnesota. In 1857, with Stephen Hanks as pilot, she raced Harris's *War Eagle* through Lake Pepin and beat her to St. Paul, arriving at 2 a.m. May 1. Burned and sank at Red Wing MN June 30, 1858 with loss of several lives.

Galena Packet *rig and tonnage unknown.* Usually *Saint Louis & Galena Packet* (which see).

Galenian *1834–1839, sidewheel 133 tons.* Built at Pittsburgh. From her home port of St. Louis she regularly made trips to the lead region, but probably did not come above. Capt. Rogers brought her into Galena Apr. 2, 1836, third boat of the season, after having already left a large freight at Dubuque. Like many Upper Mississippi R. boats, she spent her winters on the Ohio R. Burned at Bayou Plaquemine LA in March 1839.

General Brooke *1842–1849, sidewheel 143 tons.* Built at Pittsburgh: 144x20x5'2", single engine. The American Fur Co. and Capt. Joseph Throckmorton were partners in this packet. In May 1842 Throckmorton had her at St. Paul and on the St. Croix. In 1843 the boat made 7 trips between Galena and Fort Snelling. She was sold in 1845 to Joseph La Barge for $12,000 (today $285,000) for the Missouri R. where she traveled as far as Fort Union ND. Burned in the 1849 St. Louis wharf fire.

General Neville *1822–1827, sidewheel 103 tons.* Built at Pittsburgh: open hull; single engine. She was named for an aide of the Marquis de Lafayette, and originally operated out of Louisville KY. She was at Prairie du Chien in 1824, and at Fort

Snelling with Indian goods and stores prior to May 1826. In June 1825 she returned to St. Louis with furs from the Columbia Fur Co. at the St. Peters. Off registration lists 1827.

General Pike   *1840–1843, sternwheel 234 tons.* Built at Cincinnati: 172x26x5'6". This packet is often confused with the *Pike* (1838–45). Edward Durant put her on the St. Croix R. in 1840, and she likely also visited the St. Peters. In 1840 her master was John Armstrong, owner Jacob Strader. She was snagged in February 1843 and went down with loss of 3 lives. (Also see *Pike.*)

Geneva   *1848–1852, sternwheel 121 tons.* Built at Brownsville PA: 3 boilers. *Geneva* went to the Upper Mississippi and made one trip to St. Paul in 1852. She was taking wood 4 miles below Alton IL Dec. 2, 1852, when her three boilers exploded with loss of many lives including Capt. Johnson. Rebuilt, she went to the Missouri R. She was snagged and lost at Nebraska City NE in 1856. Joseph Throckmorton was master at the time of loss.

Georgetown   *1852–1855, sternwheel 183 tons.* Hull built at Line Island PA, completed at Pittsburgh: 2 boilers, engines 14's. Owned by Capt. Thomas Poe, she was snagged in the Missouri R. in October 1853, but was raised and refitted and apparently was known afterward as *New Georgetown*. She ran on the Des Moines R. and was first seen at St. Paul during 1854, running from St. Louis as an independent, "a newly furnished and elegant craft," commanded by S. G. Cabbell. She was also at Stillwater from St. Louis in October 1854. Snagged fatally at Bellefontaine Bluffs, loaded with U. S. government supplies, May 1855.

Gipsy   *1836–1841, sternwheel 79 tons.* Built at Pittsburgh. Her name is also written *Gypsy, Gipsey.* This low-water boat first ran on Rock R., advertising in 1838 to go as far as Oregon City. She was noted at Galena loading for the St. Peters in 1837 and 1838. In fall 1838 she was chartered for $450 to carry Ojibwe annuity goods from Fort Snelling to St. Croix Falls: after running aground in Lake St. Croix, she arrived at the Falls Oct. 26 1838 to meet more than 1,000 Indians. She was the third boat to ascend the St. Croix; Capt. P. Gray was her master 1838–9. For a while in 1839 she was only boat operating on the upper river because of low water. Stranded 1841 at Keokuk.

Glaucus 1   *1839–1842, sidewheel 191 tons.* Built at Pittsburgh. Capt. John Atchison took her twice to Fort Snelling in 1839. She was probably the first boat to land at the site of St. Paul that year. Part of the cargo was 6 barrels of whiskey for David Faribault; some soldiers from Fort Snelling got it and became mutinous. *Glaucus* was noted for the "stentorian" quality of her whistle. Snagged and lost near Hannibal MO August 1842.

Glaucus 2   *1849–1852, sternwheel 154 tons.* Built at West Elizabeth PA for the St. Louis & Keokuk Packet Co., she made at least one trip to St. Paul before being burned and lost at Montrose IA Mar. 30, 1852.

Globe   *1849–1856, sidewheel 211 tons.* Built at Paducah KY. Louis Robert was part owner and his nephew Nelson Robert was at times her master. In 1853–6 Capt. Haycock had her and divided her time between the Des Moines and the Minnesota rivers. She was the first boat up the Minnesota R.

in 1854. In 1855, under Capt. Edwin Bell, she carried annuity goods to the Dakota at Redwood Agency. She struck a rock within two miles of the landing and the goods had to be taken off there. The dry prairie grass caught fire, destroying most of the Indians' provisions, including 50 barrels of powder. Off lists 1856.

Golden Era *1852–1868, sidewheel 249 tons.* Built at Wheeling VA: 178x29x5.1'. Capt. Hiram Bersie had her in the Galena & Minnesota Packet Co. 1852–4. She usually connected with the *Nominee* at Galena, carrying the passengers on to St. Louis. On the 1854 Grand Excursion she carried ex-president Millard Fillmore; the passengers were so delighted with Capt. Bersie they presented him with a silver cup. By 1855 Pierce Atchison had her at St. Paul. She was in the Galena, Dunleith & Minnesota Packet Co. in 1856 and served as a troop transport during the Civil War. Sold to New Orleans 1866; dismantled 1868.

Gossamer *1850–1854, sternwheel 142 tons.* Built at McKeesport PA. In May 1854, the *St. Louis Democrat* announced: "The lightdraft steamer Gossamer is off this afternoon for the interesting territory of Minnesota. She is a neat and sterling craft." One of the lightest boats ever run in the through trade, after one trip she appears to have transferred to the Missouri. In June 1854 she was sunk rounding into the woodyard at Clarksville MO, heavily freighted with grain valued at $6–8,000 (today $130-170,000). Her commander and owner was Capt. Reid.

Governor Briggs *1845–1854, sidewheel 90 tons.* Built at St. Louis. She first ran on the Illinois R. through 1846, then transferred to the Galena trade carrying the U. S. mail. In July 1846, she was making the Galena and Potosi (WI) run, Capt. James E. Starr. She was sunk at St. Louis July 1849, but was raised and sold to Memphis interests. No longer on lists 1854.

Governor Dodge *1837?–1840, sidewheel, 219 tons.* Built at Pittsburgh. Although Lytle–Holdcamper has her build date as 1838, this steamer is documented as far as Dubuque in 1837. Off the lists by 1840.

Governor Ramsey *1849–?, sidewheel, tonnage unknown.* Single shaft. This small steamer was built at St Anthony MN by A. R. Young over the winter of 1849–50 for Capt. John Rollins to run above the Falls of St. Anthony to Sauk Rapids. The machinery came from Bangor ME. The *Ramsey* was the first steamer to operate above the falls.

Grand Prairie *1852–1857, sidewheel 261 tons.* Built at Gallipolis OH: 178x24x6'4". She began operating out of Cincinnati, then made three trips St. Louis to St. Paul in 1853, Capt. E. A. Sheble, and became a through boat to St. Paul in 1854–5. Off enrollment lists 1857.

Gray Cloud *1854–1863, sidewheel 245 tons.* Built at Elizabeth PA: 181x28'9"x5'9", 3 boilers. St. Louis was her home port. A St. Louis–St. Paul packet, she was "well calculated for low water." In July and August 1854 she delivered 300 sacks of corn, 200 of oats and 36 of apples to Stillwater, Capt. P. A. Alford, clerk Thomas B. Rhodes. In 1855 she was on the Missouri R. She was re-named *Colonel Kinsman* by the Confederates, was captured in 1862 and became the Federal *USS Kinsman*. Snagged and sunk at Berwick Bay LA in 1863 with loss of 6 lives.

Greek Slave *1849–1857, sidewheel 143 tons.* Built at Jeffersonville IN, she boasted the first steam capstan (a device for winching off sandbars). Built for the Tennessee R. trade, she had paintings on her wheelhouses of the celebrated statue "Greek Slave" by sculptor Hiram Powers. The painting was described as "very neat and chaste and very appropriate; attracts the attention of everyone." Louis Robert bought her in 1852, making her the first boat owned in St. Paul. Robert wintered her at St. Paul, so she could start the steamboat season on the Minnesota R. before the ice left L. Pepin. She made several trips to Stillwater in 1852, 18 trips Rock Island–St. Paul in 1853. In 1854 Robert sold this popular boat to the Minnesota Packet Co. and she continued in the St. Paul–St. Louis trade under Capt. George R. Melville through 1856. Off lists 1857.

Gypsey *1836–1841, sternwheel 79 tons.* Also spelled *Gipsy,* which see.

H

H. M. Rice *1854–?, 119 tons; rig unknown.* Built at St. Anthony MN. No official documentation of this steamer has been found, although it is probable she was built to run above the Falls of St. Anthony. She was noted on the Minnesota R. in 1855.

Hamburg *1849–1858, sidewheel 256 tons.* Built at Elizabeth PA: 168x26′6″x5′; transom stern; cabin on deck. This large packet was noted at Stillwater in July 1854 under Capt. Cook. She was running Dubuque–St. Paul in 1855, Capt. J. B. Estes, and St. Louis–St. Paul 1856-7, Capt. Rowe. In 1857 she arrived at St. Paul with a sawmill for South Bend (near Mankato) on the Minnesota R. She laid up at Red Wing for the winter 1857–8, was stove in the spring breakup and sank below Wacouta MN. Capt. `Obe' Eames pulled her out, put the cabin and machinery in a new hull and launched her again in 1865 as *Minnesota.*

Hawkeye *1829–1838, sidewheel 105 tons.* Better known as *Galena* (1), which see.

Helen *sidewheel 61 tons, dates unknown.* This small packet was at Galena from St. Louis in 1845 and 1846, was noted loading for the St. Peters June 1846, Capt. H. J. Sweeney serving as both master and clerk—on deck she had 1,000 bricks consigned to Churchill & Nelson at Stillwater. This is likely the steamer Capt. John W. Darrah listed as "Helen Sweeney" and may be the 1846 arrival William R. Brown calls "Heuer" (see *Heuer).*

Henrietta *1853–1860, sternwheel 179 tons.* Built at California PA: 143.5x25.5x4.8′. *Henrietta* ran Pittsburgh–Louisville briefly, then was sold to the Upper Mississippi and ran as a tramp or freelancer. Capt. C. B. Goll made two trips in 1853 to St. Paul and Stillwater, and she was a regular at St. Paul through 1859. At Stillwater in July 1854, the sheriff tried to serve Capt. Stephen Hewitt with a writ to collect for debts owed in St. Paul. *Henrietta* tried to back off but the deputy held her snubbed. Rocks were thrown. Finally a crewman cut her free and she steamed away, leaving the rope as payment along with several bloodied noses. A few days later at Guttenberg IA she was again boarded by a sheriff who was reportedly knocked senseless by a deck hand. The boat took off with him, but the crew helped him and later landed him near his home in Iowa. *Henrietta's* crew was apprehended at Muscatine and held for trial; they were released and the boat was soon back at St. Paul, despite the brouhaha. In 1854 she was advertised as a packet for the Northern Line, Capt. Gray. Off lists 1860.

Hermann *1848–1856, sidewheel 194 tons.* Built at Louisville KY and operating from that port, she collided with and sank the *Emma Watts* on the Wabash R. in 1853. In May 1854 she showed up at St. Louis loading for St. Paul and a few days later was reported sinking at Gilberts Landing, supply point on Lake Pepin for the Chippewa R. pineries. In 1856 she was running Pittsburgh to St. Louis, Capt. Kinkle. Off lists 1857.

Heroine *1832–1837, sidewheel 96 tons.* Built at Bridgeport PA. This Ohio R. boat, Capt. Orrin Smith owner and master, was at Galena in April 1835 with a large freight cargo and some 300 passengers. She broke her shafts just below the mouth of Fever R. and had to be towed up by *Wisconsin*. She was at Dubuque in 1836, Capt. Tomlin, and at Galena, the St. Peters and Fort Snelling in 1837, commanded by Capt. Hitchcock. Stranded and lost near Keokuk June 1837.

Heuer *dates, rig and tonnage unknown.* William R. Brown of Newport MN notes a boat of this name stopping in the summer of 1846. There is no other record of this name, which may be miswritten (see *Helen*).

Hibernian *1844–1848, sidewheel 152 tons.* Built at Pittsburgh and operating out of St. Louis, she was advertised for the St. Peters in 1844 and 1845, Capt. S. M. Kennett, and was on the St. Croix in 1845. Burned at St. Louis Mar. 10, 1848.

Highland Mary *1848–1856, sidewheel 158 tons.* Built at St. Louis and owned by independent Capt. John Atchison, she was often at St. Paul and Stillwater from St. Louis 1848–1850. She carried a highland lassie figurehead and sported a brass band. She was at Stillwater in May and again in July 1848, and also plied the Missouri R. In July 1849 she arrived at St. Paul with a pleasure party and a barge loaded with milk cows for the fort. By 1850 she was a regular packet from St. Louis to St. Paul but went out early that season with the death of Capt. John Atchison of cholera on board her at St. Louis. The boat was laid up; then bought in 1852 by Capt. Joseph La Barge who ran her on the lower Mississippi; later chartered by Pierre Chouteau & Co. for service on the Missouri R. She was damaged by fire at St. Louis in 1853, was finally lost in the ice at St. Louis Feb. 26, 1856.

Highland Mary No. 2 *1848–1853, sidewheel 158 tons?* Built at Wheeling VA. She ran on the Ohio R. when new; in 1849 was a ferry at St. Joseph MO conveying immigrants across the Missouri. She is probably the "Highland Mary" reported sunk that April. By 1849 John Atchison, who also owned the first *Highland Mary*, had the "No. 2" in the St. Louis–Galena trade. She was at Stillwater in fall 1849, again in April 1850. In 1849 she was one of the first St. Paul arrivals, crowded with passengers, and shared first-boat honors with *Nominee* in 1850. Sold July 1850 "to return no more" she was lost at St. Louis March 1853 in a wharf fire a that also damaged the *Dr. Franklin*.

Highlander *1842–1849, sidewheel 346 tons.* Built at Pittsburgh for the St. Louis to New Orleans trade, which she plied 1844–6 in command of Capts. Gilman and Brother, *Highlander* also ran on the Upper Mississippi. She was one of the largest there in 1848 when Capt. E. H. Gleim brought her to St. Paul. She burned at St. Louis May 1, 1849, a $14,000 ($326,000) loss.

Hindoo *1849–1855, sidewheel 199 tons.* Built at Brownsville PA. Owners Capt. William Holliday, Doc Duryea (clerk), Ross B. Hughes and W. A. W. Gault of Keokuk usually ran her Keokuk–St. Louis, but she was twice at St. Paul in 1853 under Capt. Haight, and at Stillwater in August 1854 bringing up mill and millstone for Taylor & Fox of Taylors Falls. In 1854 she was plying the Potosi trade; that June she left Potosi with 4,600 sacks of wheat plus 1,600 pigs of iron, in addition to oats and corn. She was sold to the Missouri R. to run as the Council Bluffs–Omaha ferry. Snagged and lost at Ste. Genevieve MO January 1855.

Hudson *1829–1841, sidewheel 346 tons.* Built at Pittsburgh: 151x26′3″x9′3″. Her port was first Louisville, then New Orleans. She came into the upper river trade about 1830 and was at Fort Snelling that year. According to report, she was sunk a mile below Guttenberg IA in 1841

Humboldt *1851–?, rig and tonnage unknown.* Built at Oquawka IL. The first boat to offer triweekly service on the St. Croix from Stillwater–Taylors Falls 1851–1854, *Humboldt* would stop anywhere along the river to do business. She always stopped at Marine Mills to allow the passengers to get dinner (as she had no galley) and "gave passengers a longer ride for a dollar than any other craft."

Various masters included Capt. Ericsson, Albert Eames, John Haycock and A. E. Burton. She made two trips on the Minnesota R. in 1853 and about a dozen in 1854 for her new owner C. D. Fillmore. Tiny and underpowered, she was the butt of many jokes. One passenger described her as "a drygoods box with legs standing on a floating plank." Another said her engines had "one teakettle power" and she could be stopped "by a common-sized chip floating in the water."

I

Indian Queen *1839–1845, sidewheel 137 tons.* Built at Jacksonville PA. Her first port was Pittsburgh, but by 1840 Capt. Saltmarsh had her in trade from Galena to St. Louis and also on the St Croix R. In 1841 Anson Northrop brought his family to St. Croix Falls on the *Queen*, being delayed three days while she was stuck on a St. Croix R. sandbar. That May Stillwater's first residents, Lydia Carli and family, arrived at J. R. Brown's farm on Grey Cloud Island on the *Queen*. Off lists 1845.

Indiana *1822–1829, sidewheel 130 tons.* Built at New Albany IN: 105x23′5″x5′10″. A fast boat, she left St. Louis May 13, 1824, master Silas Craig, and returned Jun. 5, 1824, making the round trip to the St. Peters in 23 days—a record for the time. She was at Fort Snelling again in 1826 and in 1827 was in the Galena–St. Louis lead trade under Capt. Culver. Capt. John Newman also commanded in 1827 and Capt. Fay in 1828. She was a strange-looking open-hold boat with her cabin aft the wheels. Off lists 1829.

Iola *1853–?, sternwheel 84 tons.* Built at Galena IL: 82x13', 25 hp engines. The second boat built at Galena to go into the Wisconsin R. trade, this small steamer was purchased in 1853 by William Constans, a St. Paul grocer, to operate on the Minnesota R., generally running between the rapids at Carver and points above. Boasted the *Galena Jeffersonian,* "It is calculated she can run when it is just a little damp." She was noted at St. Paul September 1853 and was a regular in the St. Paul–Minnesota R. trade 1854-5, Capt. Wm. H. Sargent. In 1854 she ran between St. Paul and Point Douglas, Prescott, Stillwater and Taylors Falls on the St. Croix R. She was sunk in June 1854 at Traverse des Sioux, but soon raised and Capt. R. M. Spencer had her on the Minnesota R. again in 1855.

Ione 1 *1839–1846, sidewheel 170 tons.* Built at Pittsburgh for Capt. George W. Atchison, this single engine craft was noted at Davenport and Prairie du Chien in 1839. She operated out of St. Louis on the Upper Mississippi, especially in the lead trade from Galena, Capt. James Ward, and often towed 3 keelboats, which enabled her to ship 350 tons of freight. She advertised an excursion to the St. Peters in 1840, ran Galena to St. Louis and on the St. Croix in 1842, Capt. Le Roy Dodge. She sank at Mt. Vernon, Missouri R. 1846.

Ione 2 *1853–1854, sidewheel 56 tons.* Built on Wisconsin's Fox River, this light-draft packet made 4 trips to St. Paul from St. Louis in 1853, was also on the Minnesota R. This is likely the boat reported as "Ionia" that appeared at St. Paul from the Minnesota R. in October 1853, Capt. Hall. Snagged and sunk on the Minnesota R. 1854.

Ionia *date, rig and tonnage unknown.* Probably a misprint for *Ione* (2), which see.

Iowa *1841–1845, sidewheel 112 tons.* Built at Pittsburgh. A fast boat built for the St. Louis–Galena trade, she cost Capt. Le Grande Morehouse $22,000 in 1841 (nearly $450,000 today). In 1842–3 she was a regular in the trade, making 23 trips in 1843 alone and clearing $10,000 in freight and $8,000 on passengers (in today's money totaling $400,000). She was in the Galena–Dubuque–St. Peters trade 1844-5, and advertised a trip to the Falls of St. Anthony in 1845, Capt. D. B. Morehouse. Snagged and sunk at Iowa Is. near Alton IL September 1845, a total loss.

Irene *1837–1839, sidewheel 165 tons.* Built at Pittsburgh by George W. Atchison for the Upper Mississippi, she was advertised as a "new and elegant" boat for the St. Peters her first year out in 1837. That summer Gov. Henry Dodge of Wisconsin Territory took her to Fort Snelling to negotiate a treaty with the Ojibwe. Hiram Bersie was her master in the Galena–Dubuque–St. Louis trade in 1838; she also ran as a ferry between Rock Island and Davenport. Off lists 1839.

Iron City *1844–1848, sternwheel 118 tons.* Built at Pittsburgh, she ran most of her career in the St. Louis–Galena-Dubuque trade. In November 1845 she left Galena battling her way through the ice, only to be frozen in near Keokuk. The following year Capt. J. C. Ainsworth put her in the St. Paul trade. She was at Stillwater from St. Louis in 1846 and at St. Paul in 1847. On New Year's Eve 1848 was crushed by ice as she tried to leave St. Louis, sinking to within two feet of her hurricane deck so quickly that 5 of the crew were drowned.

J

James Lyon *1853–1858, sternwheel 187 tons.* Built at Belle Vernon PA. This fine, large boat usually towed two barges. Thomas Lyon was her master in 1854, advertised for Dubuque. That year Thomas and M. S. Lyon sold her to William Holliday (captain) and W. A. W. Gault (clerk) who ran her from Potosi (outlet for Wisconsin lead mines) to St. Louis. She was noted at St. Paul from St. Louis several times in 1855–7, Capt. Blake, and in 1858. She also ran on the Missouri R. where she foundered and sank December 1858.

Jasper *1841–1845, sidewheel 83 tons.* Built at New Albany IN. *Jasper* was a regular in the Galena trade from 1841–1843. In 1843 she made 7 trips to St. Paul and also appeared on the St. Croix R. Off lists 1845.

Jenny Lind 1 *1851–1865, sidewheel 77 tons.* Built on Lake Winnebago WI: 130x24′, engines 16″ with 5′ stroke. Built as a broad-beamed lake boat with deep draft, her boiler on her keelson and a single engine, she was "a very fair running but somewhat rough looking little craft," according to one observer. She was brought through the Portage Canal to the Wisconsin R. and entered the Minnesota R. trade in July 1852 making 3 trips. After being reconstructed and lengthened at Rock Island in 1853–4 she was run as a regular packet by Capt. J. B. Estes to St. Paul and Stillwater. Failure to deliver goods to Stillwater got her embroiled in a lawsuit in 1853; when met by the sheriff at St. Paul with bills owed, she performed the usual transient's trick of cutting her cable and departing. Off lists 1865.

Jenny Lind 2 *1848–1854, sternwheel 107 tons.* Built at Zanesville OH: 132x22x4′. Daniel Hurd operated her on the Muskingum and Ohio rivers until October 1851, when she was sold to the Spaulding, Rogers & Van Order circus to replace the *Loyal Hanna*. She may be the *Jenny Lind* that was on the Des Moines R. in the early 1850s, Capt. S. Ainsworth. This boat was sold to the St. Louis & Keokuk Packet Co. in 1853, and in 1854 was a last minute addition to the Grand Excursion, making only part of the trip. Off lists 1854.

Jo Daviess *1832–1835, sidewheel 26 tons.* Built at Portage Prairie (about 3 miles from Galena IL): 90′5″x15′3″x2′. Twenty-five-year-old Smith Harris built her from the hull of the keelboat *Colonel Bumford* and an old engine his brother Scribe Harris discovered in a scrapheap on the Cincinnati levee. She may have been the first steamboat built on the upper river. She hauled lead from Galena to St. Louis, was first boat up the Wisconsin R. in 1834 with supplies and troops for Fort Winnebago, and was in the St. Peters trade. Harris sold her in 1834. Snagged and lost at Alton IL August 1835.

John J. Hardin *1845–1848, sidewheel 209 tons.* Built at West Elizabeth PA for the St. Louis–Galena–upper river trade, she generally operated from St. Louis. Burned at St. Louis March 1848.

Josephine *1826?–1829, sidewheel 57 tons.* Built at Cincinnati c1826 (one source has her built in 1827, but she was noted at the St. Peters sometime before May 1826 with military supplies). In 1828–9 she served as a packet ferrying goods between the Mississippi rapids under Capt. Joseph Clark. Capt. Clark broke ice in Fever R. to bring provisions to starving miners at Galena in February 1828 only to be frozen in until mid-March. She was noted in 1829 at Fort Armstrong with 2 barges, Capt. Michael Littleton. Burned at Buffalo Slough on the Mississippi 1829.

Julia *1846–1850, sidewheel 246 tons.* Built at Elizabeth PA. She was at St. Paul in 1846 commanded by Joseph W. Converse who sold her in 1848 to John W. Keiser of Pierre Chouteau Jr. and Co. She operated on the Missouri R. until snagged and sunk there at Bellefontaine Bend September 1850.

Julia Dean *1850–1857, sternwheel 117 tons.* Built at McKeesport PA: 138.5x24x3.8′. This packet was at Stillwater in 1853–4, at St. Paul 1855–6 and may also have been on the Des Moines R. for a time. In 1854 she had her wheelhouse blown off by a storm at Rock Island. She was lost in collision with *Rainbow* at Mount Vernon IN in 1857 with loss of 5 lives.

Justice *1851–1858, sternwheel 75 tons.* Built at West Newton PA in 1851, she ran on the Allegheny and Ohio rivers before being sold in July 1854 to the Upper Mississippi. Described as a "new packet," she appeared at St. Paul in late 1854. That year Capt. Gillim decided to run her as a regular Galena–Rock Island packet. Off lists 1858.

K

Kentucky *1849-1855, sidewheel 98 tons.* Built at Wellsville OH. She was operating on the Kentucky R. in 1850 and by 1854 was on the Upper Mississippi. She left St. Louis for St. Paul that August, was in St. Paul again in October 1854. Burned at Rock Island 1855.

Kentucky No. 2 *1851–1858, sidewheel 148* tons. Built at Evansville IN. Operating from Louisville, she ran the lower Mississippi and Missouri until 1854 when Capt. Obadiah `Obe' Eames bought her along with the *Dan Hillman* to tow rafts through Lakes Pepin and St. Croix. Eames sold her to Capt. George Rissue of Prescott, who used her as a raft tow and also to ship lime from his kiln near Prescott to St. Paul. At Rock Island in July 1855 she caught fire while landing alongside the *Prairie State,* destroying the latter. Refitted, she broke her moorings during spring ice breakup 1858, was crushed and sank on a bar one mile below Prescott WI.

Knickerbocker *1838–1839, sidewheel 169 tons.* Built at Pittsburgh. She was first boat to Dubuque from St. Louis in 1838 under Capt. Van Houten; was at Fort Snelling in June 1839 with goods for the fort sutler from Galena, Capt. E. W. Gould. James B. Eads, who later built the first bridge across the Mississippi at St. Louis, was second clerk on her. Snagged and lost at Cairo IL December 1839.

L

Lady Franklin *1850–1856, sidewheel 206 tons.* Built at Wheeling VA: 180x27x4′6″. A beautiful sidewheeler built for the Cincinnati & St. Louis Mail Line, her first trip to St. Paul was in June 1851. As a Minnesota Packet Co. boat she was commanded by E. H. Gleim in 1853 and took part in the Grand Excursion in June 1854 under Capt. Le Grande Morehouse. She replaced the wrecked *Nominee* that October, Pierce Lodwick, master. In May 1855 Capt. J. W. Malin brought 800 passengers to St. Paul from St. Louis on her. Snagged and sunk at the foot of Coon Slough on the same snag that sunk the *Nominee* October 1856 with loss of 5 lives. The wrecks lay together there 40 years.

Lady Washington *1828–1832, sidewheel 121 tons.* Built at Pittsburgh, her first port was New Orleans. In 1829 she was at Galena from Pittsburgh, Capt. John Shallcross, a government charter loading for Fort Snelling. This sidewheel packet may be confused with the barge *Lady Washington,* which was towed by the *Saint Louis & Galena Packet* (which see); it is also possible this steamboat was the Galena Packet. Snagged and lost January 1832. The barge disappears in 1830.

Lamartine *1848–1856, sidewheel 174 tons.* Built at Elizabeth PA. She went to the Upper Mississippi as a tramp in 1850, making several trips to St. Paul that year. That May Capt. J. W. Marsh had her within a mile of the Falls of St. Anthony. Because of high water in 1850 she was able to ascend the Apple (WI) R. and also sail into downtown Stillwater up to the Minnesota House on Main St. She was at St. Paul 1851-2, Capt. Sam Harlow. In November 1851 she was attached at Stillwater for some old claim, but managed to slip her hawser, leaving it and a deckhand behind, and "showed a clean pair of heels down the lake." Refitted in 1852, she was chartered to take a survey party to establish the northern boundary of Iowa, under Capt. Andrew Talcott. Lost in ice at St. Louis February 1856.

Lawrence *1824–1827, sidewheel 122 tons.* Built at Cincinnati. Her first port was New Orleans, but she soon was plying in the Galena lead trade. In May 1826 she was the first supply boat to Fort Snelling and the first steamboat to make an excursion to the Falls of St. Anthony—Capt. D. F. Reeder took his guests to within 3½ miles of the cataract, where some of the party played games, others danced to a military band. In early 1827 she was running Louisville–St. Louis–St. Peters, Reeder master. Off lists in 1827. James Hall lists her as "worn out."

Lewis F. Linn *1844–1852, sidewheel 163 tons.* Built at Pittsburgh. Capt. S. M. Kennett brought her new to St. Louis from Pittsburgh in March 1844, and she became a regular on the Upper Mississippi. She was at the St. Peters from Galena in 1844, on the St. Croix the same year, and advertised for trip to the Falls of St. Anthony in May 1846. Reported snagged at the head of St. Charles Is., Missouri R., 1848–9. Off lists 1852.

Lightfoot *1845–1858, sidewheel 145 tons.* Single engine. Built at Cincinnati as a lock-boat, with narrow shape to pass through the Louisville locks, she had a long, sharp bow that got her the nickname `Gar.' Capt. Keeler Harris had her in trade with *Time & Tide*, another Harris boat, on the upper river. She was an excursion boat from Galena to Fort Snelling in 1845 and in 1846 was running Galena–Stillwater–Mendota under Capt. A. G. Montford. Capt. Harris brought her in first to Galena 1847. She made 14 trips on the Missouri R. in 1848, Capt. William Phelps, and was later sold to the Illinois R. trade. In 1857 she was hauling stone for the St. Louis railroad bridge. Reported burned at St. Louis 1858.

Little Dove *1845–1851, sidewheel 76 tons.* Built at St. Louis for a cost of $5,500 ($131,000), she was a regular in the Galena–St. Peters trade in 1846, Capt. H. Hoskins. Off lists 1851.

Little Missouri *1846–1848, sidewheel 198 tons.* Built at Cincinnati for Capt. Robert Wright, *Little Missouri* traded out of St. Louis and was at St. Paul at least once in the 1840s. Wright took her to the Missouri R. where she was snagged and sunk in April 1848 at a location later known as Little Missouri Bend.

Loyal Hanna *1836–1843, sternwheel 76 tons.* Built at Pittsburgh. Sometimes written *Loyalhanna*, she was an Illinois R. packet in 1840 when she was advertised in the Galena papers for a pleasure excursion to Fort Snelling and the St. Peters. Off lists 1843.

Luella *1851–1856, sidewheel 162 tons.* Built at Nashville KY. Her engines came from a New Orleans boat and were too large for *Luella,* but this caused her to be speedy. Owned by the Galena, Dunleith & St. Paul Packet Co., she first came to Stillwater and St. Paul in fall 1852, replacing *Martha No. 2* (Capt. Stephen Hewitt). She made 7 trips to St. Paul in 1853, was the first boat through from St. Louis in 1854 (Capt. Charles Morrison), and a regular Rock Island to St. Paul packet 1854-5 (Capt. Sam Harlow). In September 1853 she brought up the Winnebago and Ojibwe annuity goods. In fall 1854 she was sold to S. H. Boyce and others of St. Paul. She was dismantled at Dunleith in 1856 after a brief, ignominious career as a floating "gunboat" (whorehouse).

Lunette *1852–1853, sidewheel 166 tons.* Built at McKeesport PA. A swift and elegant little low-water boat drawing only 18″, *Lunette* made her first and last appearance at St. Paul from St. Louis in September 1853. She was built for and operated by Capt. John B. Davis, who intended making her a regular in the trade. However, when she was loading at St. Louis for her second trip on Oct. 15, 1853, she caught fire and burned, a total loss.

Lynx *1844–1849, sidewheel 124 tons.* Built at Cincinnati: 124x20x4′6″. First registered May 1844, she was purchased by several agents of Pierre Chouteau Jr. & Co. to assure regular weekly service to the Minnesota R. She ran from Galena to Prairie du Chien, St. Peters and the St. Croix, was noted landing supplies for Wabasha's band at the site of Winona in 1844. First captain and part-owner was W. H. Hooper, later John Atchison. She was first through Lake Pepin ice in 1846, and the following year took an excursion of notables to Fort Snelling and Minnehaha Falls. She sank in 1844 and was raised; snagged and was lost near Clarksville MO 1849.

M

Maid of Iowa *1842–1846, sidewheel 60 tons.* Built at August IA. This small packet was operating out of Galena in 1845, plying a regular route to Dubuque, Potosi, Cassville, Prairie du Chien and up the Wisconsin R. to Portage. There she connected with (yet-another) *Enterprise* on the Fox R., giving a through line to Green Bay. Off lists 1846.

Malta *1839–1841, sidewheel 114 tons.* Built at Pittsburgh: 140x22x5′, double engines, fire pump & hose. Built at a cost of $18,000 (today nearly $350,000), her owners were Capt. Joseph Throckmorton and Pierre Chouteau Jr. of St. Louis, and her cargo was often furs and Indian trade goods. She arrived at Fort Snelling July 22, 1839, with several dignitaries and annuity goods for the Dakota on board; on the 24th she went round to

Lake St. Croix so the passengers could visit the late Indian battleground (Battle Hollow in Stillwater). She also made a pleasure trip to the Falls of St. Anthony in 1840, Wm. P. Gorman master. She was loaded with furs when Throckmorton ran her on a snag in the Missouri R. in 1841—total loss.

Mandan *1819–1825, sidewheel 127 tons.* Built at New Albany IN. Heavily loaded with military supplies and carrying Brig. Gen. Winfield Scott, she left St. Louis Apr. 5, 1824, for Fort St. Anthony (Fort Snelling) "with her guards dripping." She returned to St. Louis in 62½ hours running time—Capt. William Linn said he thought he could make the 1500-mile round trip in 10 days. Stranded near Vicksburg November 1824, finally snagged and wrecked January 1825.

Mansfield *1854–1858, sternwheel 166 tons.* Built at Belle Vernon PA, she went immediately to the upper river trade operating from St. Louis. In May 1854 she was loaded with 250 tons for Dubuque, but was held up at Keokuk because of low water and may not have got above the rapids. That fall she was running the mail at Louisville, Capt. R. M. Wade. She was in the Stillwater and St. Paul trade in 1856-7, and was logged on the Missouri R. in 1858. Snagged and lost at White Cloud NE? August 1858.

Martha No. 2 *1849–1860, sidewheel 180 tons.* Built at Shousetown PA to replace Capt. Joseph La Barge's boat *Martha,* lost in the great fire at St. Louis 1849. She was logged at St. Paul April 1851 from St. Louis with a large load for the Red River Settlement (Winnipeg); was also at Stillwater that October, Edmund O'Flaherty, captain. She made 7 trips from Galena to St. Paul in 1852, was noted at Nelson WI with goods for Chippewa R. pineries 1854, and plied the Illinois R 1856–7. Off lists 1860.

Mary C *1852–1858, sternwheel 157 tons.* Built at Rockingham IA for Capt. Coleman, who owned the *Caleb Cope,* and named for his daughter, she came to the Upper Mississippi in 1853 to tow log rafts through Lakes Pepin and St. Croix. She was at St. Paul in 1853 and 1854, and at Stillwater from Moline IL in June 1854, Capt. J. E. Davidson. St. Louis papers called her "a snorter to go." In September 1854 H. A. Forse was master. She was on the Missouri R. in 1856 and 1858. Burned below Davenport in the winter of 1858–9.

Mattie Wayne *1852–1858, sidewheel 300 tons.* Built at Cincinnati and originally a Cincinnati packet, she was running to St. Paul, Capt. J. W. Davis, by 1854. In 1856 Capt. Samuel Owings ran her as a transient or "wild" boat from St. Louis to St. Paul. She was damaged by fire at St. Louis in 1855. Dismantled at Cairo in 1858, her hull was turned into a wharfboat.

Mechanic *1823–1832, sidewheel 116 tons.* Built at Marietta OH. This small single-engine boat built by Capt. Hugh White ran Galena–St. Louis in 1826-7 and 1830. She was noted at Prairie du Chien in April 1826. One account says she was at Fort Snelling with government supplies in 1829. In 1832 she hit a boulder, thereafter called "Mechanic Rock," while landing at Montrose IA. She was raised, but was stranded and lost the same year.

Mendota *1844–1848, sidewheel 157 tons.* Built at Cincinnati. She ran on the Upper Mississippi out of Galena, Capt. Robert A. Reilly, master; was reported at the St. Peters from Galena 1844; was on the St. Croix in 1845. Snagged and raised October 1847; snagged and lost at Ste. Genevieve MO January 1848.

Minnesota *1849–1862, sidewheel 149 tons.* Built at Elizabeth PA under direction of Capt. Richard C. Gray for the Northern Line, she went to the Upper Mississippi and became a transient in the Galena–St. Paul trade. She was at St. Paul 1849 and 1851 under Capt. R. A. Reilly, and later ran on the Minnesota R. In 1850 Orrin Smith was master; in 1852 E. H. Gleim. Off lists 1862.

Minnesota Belle *1849–1862, sternwheel 225 tons.* Built at Belle Vernon PA: 170′ long, 38 staterooms. Capt. G. S. Humberstone bought this well-furnished packet in 1854 to replace *Clarion* in the Minnesota R. trade. She featured luxurious touches, such as cut-glass chandeliers and oil paintings on the stateroom doors. On her first trip to St. Paul from Pittsburgh she was received with three hearty cheers at the landing. In May she carried up troops from Rock Island for Fort Ridgely. Capt. Humberstone had staked out a townsite on the Minnesota R. and started for it in May 1854 from St. Louis, loaded with immigrants, but the boat failed to get over the rapids at Carver and the captain abandoned townsite speculation in disgust. For a while she ran between Keokuk and Rock Island, connecting with *Gray Cloud* from St. Louis, but she was back on the St. Croix in November 1854 and the following season. By 1857 the *Belle* was in the St. Louis–St. Paul trade, Capt. Thomas B. Hill. Two years later she went to the Northern Line, same trade, same master. Snagged and lost at Liverpool IL Mar. 28, 1862.

Missouri *1828–1831, sidewheel 110 tons.* Built at Phillipsburg PA: 117x20x5′. She arrived at Fort Snelling commanded by Capt. A. Gros in 1828, having been chartered by the government to transport troops from Forts Snelling, Crawford and Armstrong to new posts on the frontier. She was noted leaving Jefferson Barracks in April with Col. John McNeil and 8 companies of infantry destined for the Upper Mississippi. Later William B. Culver was master. In her first year she "struck a snag and sank immediately" in the Mississippi, but was raised and soon "ready to commence running." Snagged and lost in 1831.

Missouri Fulton 1 *sidewheel, dates & tonnage unknown.* This single engine boat is probably the steamer Indian agent Taliaferro records as *Fulton,* which was at Fort Snelling prior to May 26, 1826. She was advertised at Galena for the St. Peters June 1827. In early 1828 Alvah Culver was her captain; Capt. Joseph Clark took over later in the season. It is unlikely she survived long enough to be the *Missouri Fulton* that was active in 1836–7.

Missouri Fulton 2 *1836–1839, sidewheel 120 tons.* Built at Cincinnati. First boat to Fort Snelling in 1836, she arrived May 8 with the new commander, Col. Davenport. That year Orrin Smith was her master and he had her in the Galena–Dubuque–St. Peters trade. She was advertised for a "fashionable tour" to the St. Peters in1837. A card signed by 40 passengers commended Capt. I. Perrin on the success of the trip and the gentlemanly conduct of the officers and crew. In September 1838 she was reported sunk below St. Louis. Off lists 1839.

Monona *1843–1847, sidewheel 173 tons.* Built at St. Louis. Capt. Nick Wall had her in the St. Louis–Galena trade 1845, in which she held the speed record; in 1846 she was running Galena–St. Peters, Capt. E. H. Gleim. She sank on the Missouri R. Oct. 30, 1846, was raised, and continued to ply Galena–St. Louis through the 1847 season, Capt. Ludlow Chambers. Snagged and lost at Chester IL October 1847.

Monsoon *1839–1842, sidewheel 171 tons.* Built at Cincinnati: 152x21.3x5.6', home port St. Louis. She was noted at Davenport May 1839 with recruits for Fort Crawford at Prairie du Chien. In May 1840 she was advertising a pleasure excursion from Louisville to the St. Peters and the Falls of St. Anthony leaving Jun. 6, C. G. Pearce, master—a "splendid, safe and commodious passenger steamboat." Off lists by 1842.

Montauk *1847–1849, sidewheel 175 tons.* Built at St. Louis, she was noted at Galena from St. Louis in October 1847. She towed a barge that in April 1848 sprang a leak on the Rock Island Rapids and damaged about $25,000 worth of goods (over half a million). Capt. Reilly had her in the St. Louis–St. Peters trade that year; she was at Stillwater in September 1848 with a freight that included 1,259 lbs. of drugs consigned to Churchill & Nelson. An unlucky boat, in May 1849 she arrived at Prairie du Chien having lost all cargo in an accident. She burned in the great fire at St. Louis May 1849, a $24,000 loss.

Montello *1854–1860, sternwheel 50 tons.* Built at New London WI: single engine and stack. This small, rough-looking boat was built over the hull of a barge with no boiler deck. Bought in 1854 by Joseph R. Brown for $1,500 ($32,000) for service on the Minnesota R., she operated mostly above the Little Rapids and ran with fair regularity between Carver and Traverse des Sioux, supplementing the *Black Hawk, Humboldt* and others plying below. In 1855 she made one trip to St. Paul, then ran on the St. Croix carrying passengers and freight between Stillwater and Taylors Falls. She sank in 1860 and was dismantled. A. S. Albright of Sioux City purchased the hull; the engine went into another boat. Her bell is in the J. R. Brown Minnesota Center in Henderson MN.

Mungo Park *1841–1845, sidewheel 94 tons.* Built at Pittsburgh, her unusual name is that of a Scottish explorer. Her port of registration was St. Louis, but she operated first mostly on the Illinois R. In 1843 Capt. R. A. Reilly had her at Fort Snelling with government supplies. She was on the St. Croix in 1844, and that year took Socrates Nelson and wife from Hennepin MN to St. Louis for $15 (not cheap—over $350 today). She was a regular Galena–St. Louis packet in 1845, but was lost that year between Alton and St. Louis.

N

N. P. Hawks *1841–1847, sternwheel 49 tons.* Better known as *Rock River,* which see.

Navigator *1850–1856, sternwheel 154 tons.* Built at Brownsville PA by Capt. William Dan for the Ohio R., she was sold to the St. Louis–St. Paul trade where she ran 1854–5 under Capts. A. T. Champlin and J. B. Davis. She called at Stillwater from St. Louis September 1854 with boxes of marble for Short & Proctor, and landed many tons of freight at Prescott "when the officers did not care to make the run to Stillwater." She set a new record as last boat into St. Paul Nov. 23, 1854, and plied the Missouri R. in 1856 until she was sunk on the Mississippi between Alton and St. Louis.

New Brazil *1842–1847, sidewheel 166 tons.* Better known as *Brazil* (2), which see.

New Georgetown *1852–1855, sternwheel 183 tons.* Better known as *Georgetown,* which see.

New Haven *1841–1847, sidewheel 87 tons.* Built at Pittsburgh. This small packet was first noted on the upper river at Galena loading freight for St. Louis in November 1844. In 1845 she was a regular Galena–Dubuque–Potosi packet (Potosi WI was the outlet for the Mineral Point lead mines), George L. King master. She was at St. Paul and Stillwater in 1845, was last noted at Galena June 1846. Foundered January 1847 at Wood River IL.

New Lucy *1852–1857, sidewheel 416 tons.* Built at St. Louis. She was said to be the fastest boat on the river and was certainly one of the biggest on the upper Mississippi. Capt. William Conley made at least one trip as far as Lake Pepin, where she was seen in May 1854 bound up at Read's Landing. She may have proved too large for the upper river during that low-water year—later she was reported arriving in St. Louis from the Missouri R. She caught fire at St. Louis in January 1853, was rebuilt and finally burned at De Witt MO November 1857.

New Saint Croix *1854–?, sternwheel tonnage unknown.* Built at Oquawka IL for the St. Croix R. trade in 1854 by Capt. `Obe' Eames, she had a new hull, using machinery from *Enterprise* (an Ohio R. boat of the name). In the summer of 1854 Eames

had the whole business of the St. Croix. In 1855–7 she ran on the Chippewa R. La Crosse to Eau Claire. She was sunk by ice on Lake Pepin in April 1857, raised and towed to St. Paul and again put into service. Final disposition unknown.

New Saint Paul *1852–1857, sidewheel 265 tons.* Built at Wheeling VA: 220x36x6', 3 boilers, engines 21's, 7' stroke (dimensions as rebuilt). A luxury boat and a much heralded entry brought by Keeler Harris into the St. Paul trade in 1852, she made 7 trips from Galena and 4 from St. Louis that season as the *Saint Paul.* Her cost to the Harrises is reported as $25,000 (equivalent today to over $580,000). The cabin was elegantly furnished with tapestry carpet, gilded cornices and mahogany furniture to attract the passenger trade, but she proved too slow and too deep draft and they soon sold her. In 1853 she was at St. Paul with a load of merry excursionists; in June 1854 she was at Stillwater for Rock Island; in 1854–5 at St. Paul for St. Louis, owner and captain James L. Bissell. She was rebuilt at New Albany in 1855–6 and her paddleboxes lettered *New Saint Paul.* Bissell was master when she was snagged and sank on the Missouri R. August 1857, boat and cargo a total loss. (Also see *Saint Paul.*)

Newton Waggoner *1848–1855, sternwheel 105 tons.* Built at Elizabeth PA. Her home port was St. Louis, but she ran regularly between Galena and Portage on the Wisconsin R., the first regular packet on that river. In 1849 the *Danube* reported meeting her at Hampton IL where she had "struck on St. Louis Rock and knocked a hole in her bottom." She was repaired, but disappears off the lists in 1855.

Nimrod *1844–1850, sidewheel 210 tons.* 156x25.8 x5.7′. Built at St. Louis for Joseph Throckmorton, Pierre Chouteau Jr. and John B. Sarpy of the Fur Co., she replaced *Omega* on the Missouri R. under Capt. Joseph La Barge. In 1845 Capt. Throckmorton made a few trips to the St. Peters and Stillwater with her, then bought *Cecilia* to finish the season. Capt. Dennis had her on the Upper Mississippi in 1846. She was sold to New Orleans concerns and lost there in 1850.

Nominee *1848–1854, sidewheel 212 tons.* Built at Shousetown PA (hull), completed Pittsburgh 1848. Built for the Ohio R., where she ran in 1849, she was sold to Orrin Smith who put her in the St. Paul trade 1850–4. A passenger called her "the finest boat on the Upper Mississippi." Smith was a pious and temperate man, who always laid her up Sundays and allowed no card playing. In July 1851 *Nominee* took Wabasha's warriors to the treaty making at Traverse des Sioux on the Minnesota R. She was a fast boat, was first through Lake Pepin 1851, 1852 & 1854, and in 1853 beat Rufus Ford's huge *Die Vernon* to Dubuque. That year Capt. Russell Blakeley made 29 trips from Galena to St. Paul and St. Croix with her. *Nominee* was a regular at Stillwater and also at Marine, usually towing a barge. In October 1850 she hit a snag and sank her barge, sending to the bottom a freight of pork, flour, oats, whiskey, dry goods and a large threshing machine. She was snagged and lost at Britts Landing IA in 1854.

O

Oakland *1853–1859, sternwheel 141 tons.* Built at California PA: 142x26.7x4′. A light-draft packet owned by Charles S. Morrison and Keokuk interests, she operated on the Upper Mississippi from St. Louis. She was noted at Stillwater August 1854 and at St. Paul 1854–8, Capt. C. S. Morrison, and also ran on the Des Moines R. In the open winter of 1854 she was one of the few boats operating between Keokuk to St. Louis and "simply coined money." Laid up and dismantled after her last run in spring 1859.

Ocean Wave *1845–1851, sidewheel 205 tons.* Built at St. Louis for the St. Louis–Keokuk trade by Capt. Barton Able. She was at St. Paul commanded by Capt. Dan Able in 1848 and that fall was running charters on the Ohio. In 1849 she carried dignitaries to the inauguration of Zachary Taylor. Burned August 1851 at Louisville KY.

O'Connell *1833–1836, sidewheel 107 tons.* Built at Pittsburgh. Reported to have been at Fort Snelling in 1834, T. Otis Reynold commanding, she was advertised as a St. Louis–Galena–Dubuque–Potosi packet in 1835. Bishop Mathias Loras arrived in Dubuque on the *O'Connell*. Snagged and lost July 1836 at Trinity KY.

Odd Fellow *1845-1848, sidewheel 97 tons.* Built at Smithland KY. She at first operated out of Nashville, but also operated on the Upper Mississippi out of St. Louis; noted at Dubuque May 1848, Capt. Klein. Stranded at Diamond Is. LA December 1848.

Oella *1848–1850, sidewheel 77 tons.* Built at Cincinnati. A boat of this name (*Oella No. 2*) is listed by John W. Darrah as being on the St. Croix R. in the 1840s. A bill of lading shows *Oella* at Stillwater July 1848 from St. Louis with 20 barrels of lime for Churchill & Nelson. She is also logged at St. Paul in 1853, but this last may be a misreading of *Luella*. Reportedly snagged and lost on the Lower Mississippi December 1850.

Olive Branch *1833–?, sidewheel 76 tons.* Built at Pittsburgh. She appeared in the Galena trade in 1834; was first arrival at Galena Apr. 1, 1836; was at Dubuque that May under Capt. R. M. Strother. In June 1837 she was at Dubuque loading for St. Louis, Capt. Holcomb. Missionary to the Dakota Stephen R. Riggs on his way to the St. Peters and his mission on the Minnesota R. was a passenger on her in 1837. It is not known what happened to her.

Omega *1840–1849, sidewheel 144 tons.* Built at Pittsburgh; 142'10"x21'6". She was at Galena loading for the St. Peters in the spring of 1840, Capt. Joseph Sire, pilot Joseph La Barge. Built for and owned by the American Fur Co., part of her freight was Indian trade supplies for Henry Sibley at Mendota. She was later on the Missouri R., in 1843 taking John J. Audubon and party of other naturalists up that river. Replaced by *Nimrod* in 1844. Dismantled in 1849.

Oneota *sidewheel, dates and tonnage unknown.* A sidewheel boat of this name was at Muscatine in 1850 and is noted plying on the Wisconsin R. with *Enterprise* (3) from Galena and Dubuque to Portage, Capt. Tuffly, in 1851.

Osceola *1854–1857, sidewheel 65 tons.* Built at Osceola WI 1854 (hull) and completed at Davenport IA: 100x18'. Built on the St. Croix R. by Humes & Cummings, she was towed to Davenport where the machinery was installed. She was the first boat built in the St. Croix valley and was designed specifically for the St. Croix R. trade. Although she was frequently at St. Paul, she made only one trip on the St. Croix—the 100' boat drew too much water and was sold to run between Rock Island and Muscatine IA. She sank in the Mississippi below Rock Island in 1857.

Osprey *1842–1848, sidewheel 128 tons.* Built at Pittsburgh. She usually ran St. Louis to Galena, but was at St. Paul in 1842, Capt. N. W. Parker, and also in 1845–6. She was hired by the government to bring annuity goods to the Indians. In 1847 she grounded on the Rock Island rapids and was dismantled where she lay.

Oswego *1847–1852, sidewheel 187 tons.* Built at Brownsville PA. This transient trader's first trip was in July 1848 and she immediately went to the Upper Mississippi, Capt. Bartlett. She was at St. Paul in November 1851, also left goods at Nelson WI and Stillwater that trip. Her arrival at Galena Nov. 26, 1851, through floating ice was recorded with some astonishment. Snagged and lost at Chester IL February 1852.

Otter *1840–1849, sidewheel 92 tons.* Built at Cincinnati: 128x18x4'3", single engine. Built by Daniel Smith Harris and designed especially to compete with boats in the American Fur Co. trade, she cost $12,000 ($250,000 today) and netted Harris $10,000 ($210,000) per year her first 3 years. In the Galena–St. Paul trade 1841–7, she was commanded by Smith Harris and his brother Scribe, with Meeker Harris as engineer and brother Jack as bartender and cub pilot. She was first boat to St. Paul in 1843–5, last boat out in 1840–1, and was also on the St. Croix River. In fall 1843 she landed at Stillwater laden with irons and machinery for the first sawmill (Stillwater Lumber Co.), and in 1844 was noted on Lake St. Croix attempting to raft a large lot of logs. That season she broke a shaft, but the inducements to Capt. Harris to make one more trip were so great that she was run up to St. Paul with but one wheel and barely escaped the ice. She collided with *Atlas* in fall 1846, killing one passenger. Sold 1848 to Capt. Darrel Cook, she was sunk on the Wisconsin R. the next year. Her engines were placed in *Tiger*.

P

Palmyra *1835-1838, sidewheel 101 tons.* Built at Pittsburgh: 129′x17′4″x5′; transom stern & cabin above deck; single engine. Owner and captain George B. Cole had her to Prairie du Chien in May 1836, then brought a pleasure party of 30 ladies and gentlemen to the Falls of St. Anthony that June, following up with a trip 3 miles up the Minnesota R. She was first into Galena 1837, Capt. E. H. Gleim, was a Galena–St. Louis packet that year, then turned independent. *Palmyra* is the first boat known to have been on the St. Croix R. In July 1838 Capt. W. Middleton brought her to Fort Snelling with notice of the Indian treaty ratification that opened the St. Croix valley to settlement. She had on board mill machinery and millwright Calvin Tuttle, which she delivered to St. Croix Falls on her return trip. Stranded and lost at Rock Island November 1838, one life lost.

Paragon *1830–1838, sidewheel 89 tons.* Built at Ripley OH: 115′6″x17′3″x5′. Her home port was Cincinnati but she was at Fort Snelling at least once, in the spring of 1833, with supplies and commanding officer Maj. John Bliss. She was also on the Missouri R. Off lists 1838.

Paris *1848–1853, sidewheel 249 tons.* Built at Freedom PA for the Ohio R., she soon became a St. Louis–Peoria packet on the Illinois and, according to one source, was at Stillwater in 1849—a very large boat for any of those rivers. Off lists 1853.

Pavilion *1836–1839, sidewheel 83 tons.* Built at Pittsburgh: single engine. Capt. James R. Lafferty and later T. H. Griffiths ran her in the Galena–St. Peters trade. One of first arrivals at Galena, March 1837, she was advertised that May for an excursion to the Falls of St. Anthony, also carried missionary Stephen R. Riggs from Galena to Fort Snelling. In summer 1837 Indian agent Lawrence Taliaferro chartered her to transport a Dakota delegation from the St. Peters to Pittsburgh, en route to Washington DC for treaty making. That fall she ascended the Des Moines R. to Fort Dodge. Still advertised for the St. Peters in August 1839; final disposition unknown.

Pearl *1845–1852, sternwheel 64 tons.* Built at West Elizabeth PA. She started life on the Illinois R., then became one of the smallest regular packets on the Upper Mississippi, running St. Louis to Galena through 1847, Capt. Ed Montgomery. In October 1847 she was at Stillwater, Capt. John A. Armstrong, loading for the St. Peters. In 1848 she ran Galena–St. Peters and made trips to St. Croix Falls stopping at Osceola and Marine. In spring 1848 she was blown ashore with the ice at the site of Lake City on Lake Pepin and had to be pulled off by Keeler Harris's sternwheeler, probably *Lightfoot*. Her early arrival at Fort Snelling that year merited an artillery salute. Off lists 1852.

Pennsylvania   *1837–1842, sidewheel 134 tons.* Built at Pittsburgh. This Ohio R. boat arrived at Fort Snelling from Pittsburgh Jun. 1, 1839, with Gen. John Wool on a tour of inspection of the western forts, Capt. Stone, master. Off lists 1842.

Pike   *1838–1845, sidewheel 294 tons.*   Built at Jeffersonville IN: 175x25x7′. Her first home port was Cincinnati; she is often confused with the *General Pike* (1840–3). On Sep. 9, 1839, she arrived at Fort Snelling from Covington KY with 80 recruits, was back a week later with 100 more troops from Prairie du Chien. She was on the upper river in 1840 when she was advertised for sale by Chouteau & McKenzie. Off lists 1845.

Pioneer 1   *1825–183?, sidewheel 199 tons.* Built at Cincinnati. One source says she was at Fort Snelling in 1836 (there are several arrivals that year not named by Lawrence Taliaferro). The steamboat built in 1825 soon disappears from the record; however, she may have been rebuilt in the 1830s. There are at least 30 steamboats that have carried the name *Pioneer*.

Pioneer 2   *1848–185?, sidewheel 89 tons.* Built at Louisville. This boat is known only from a comment of W. H. C. Folsom that she was on the St. Croix in 1854.

Pizarro   *1838–1839, sidewheel 107 tons.* Built at Cincinnati: 133x20′. Built for the Harrises of Galena at a cost of $16,000 (worth over $300,000

today) to operate on the upper river, she was captained by Smith and Scribe Harris. She was described as "commodious" and boasted the first fire pump and hose attached to her main engine. In 1839 she made a festive 4th of July excursion to Cassville complete with a band, dinner and provisions for dancing. Burned at St. Louis December 1839.

Planet   *1830–1836, sidewheel 81 tons.* Built at Cincinnati. She was brand new when the army hired her to bring a delegation of Sauk, Fox, Iowa and Otoe to Prairie du Chien to discuss peace making with the Dakota. A detachment of troops accompanied them. *Planet* operated mostly below Galena. Off lists 1836.

Plough Boy   *1848–1848, sidewheel 248 tons.* Built at St. Louis: 126x29′, 3 boilers. Also known as *Plow Boy*. Her home port was St. Louis. She made at least one trip to St. Paul before going to the Missouri R., Capt. McKee. She was snagged and sunk in October of her maiden year above Providence MO.

Prairie Bird   *1845–1851, sidewheel 213 tons.* Built at St. Louis, she cost Capt. John Vandergraft $17,000 ($380,000). He sold her to Capt. Nick Wall who ran her St. Louis to St. Peters in 1846–7, taking her also on the St. Croix most trips. She was on the Illinois in 1848. Snagged and lost at Keithsburg IL May 21, 1851.

Prairie State   *1850–1855, sternwheel 287 tons.* Built at Griggstown IL and named for the state, she originally ran on the Illinois R. In July 1854 she was in St. Paul owned by the St. Louis and Keokuk Packet Co. carrying a pleasure party of 80 and captained by Dan Able. A grand ball was held at the St. Louis Hotel for the guests. She was lost in a fire at St. Louis July 1855 that also destroyed a sawmill; the burned mill was bought by two thrifty Germans, Frederick Weyerhaeuser and Frederick Denkmann, who started a business there that became the Weyerhaeuser lumber company.

Pre-emption *1840–1848?, sidewheel 181 tons.* Built at Cincinnati: 162x26x4'3". Built by the Harris brothers and owned in partnership with merchants of St. Louis and Louisiana MO, she was run by Scribe Harris out of St. Louis, and was on the St. Croix R. at least once during the 1848 season. Supposedly she was snagged and lost in 1842 at Commerce MO. However, a boat of this name was enrolled at Cincinnati and St. Louis in 1844, so the wreck may have been rebuilt.

Q

Queen of the Yellow Banks *1850?–1853?, sternwheel 20 tons.* 40' long. A "little pet of a steamboat" that looked, according to one observer, "like two wannigans with a pilot's wheel stuck between." She was brought to the St. Croix by Capt. Al Eames and gave tri-weekly service between Stillwater and Taylors Falls for 3 months in 1852 at $1 the round trip (approximately $23 today). Then she was taken south and sold.

Quincy *1836–1838?, sidewheel 117 tons.* Built at Pittsburgh in 1836, *Quincy* began operations at St. Louis, shipping to the lead region. She was noted at Dubuque that May loading for St. Louis, Capt. Cameron. She is not registered in 1838. However, a boat named *Quincy* was in the Galena trade in 1840; if it is the same, she may have survived.

R

R. A. Riley *dates, rig and tonnage unknown.* This boat, obviously named for Capt. Robert A. Reilly of St. Louis, was advertised for St. Paul from St. Louis in 1849; it's not certain she ever made the trip.

Rambler *1823–1830, sidewheel 118 tons.* Built at Beaver PA. At first operating from Nashville TN on the Cumberland River, she was chartered by the army to haul supplies to Fort Snelling in September 1823, Capt. Bruce commanding, making her the second boat to attempt the upper river. When she left the St. Peters she took down two Swiss families from the Selkirk Colony (Winnipeg).

Rapids *1839–1843, sidewheel 109 tons.* Built at Pittsburgh. Capt. Kennett ran this steamer in the St. Louis–Galena–Dubuque lead trade in 1840. She may have started north a little early, as she was reported in March 1840 stuck in the ice at Bloomington IA. Off lists 1843.

Raritan *1840-1846, sidewheel 138 tons.* Built at Sharpsburg PA. Capt. Russell Blakeley says she was in the upper Mississippi trade under Capt. Rogers, and she is noted at Galena in 1846. Off lists that year.

Rebus *dates, rig and tonnage unknown.* Capt. Russell Blakeley says she was in the St. Paul trade during the 1854 season, but no other reference has been found.

Red Rover *1828 – 1830, 50 tons, rig unknown.* Built at Pittsburgh. Capt. Joseph Throckmorton had this small steamer in the Galena lead trade 1828–30, and she thrived as a low-water boat on the upper river. She was at Fort Snelling in 1828; in 1829 despite very low water she brought Indian treaty commissioners to Prairie du Chien, later returned with annuity goods and brought the delegation home. She was noted arriving at Galena April 1830 laden with plank, 19 cabin and 125 deck passengers and 537 packages, bales and barrels. That year she was hired to return a delegation of Dakota from Prairie du Chien to their upriver villages. Throckmorton and Capt. Shallcross formed the first cooperative association on the upper river in 1830; *Red Rover* operated above the rapids and Shallcross's *Chieftain* carried the cargoes on below.

Red Wing *1846–1849, sidewheel 142 tons.* Built at Cincinnati: 147x24x4.5'. First registered March 1846 as a Galena packet, she was in the St. Louis–Galena trade 1846–8 making occasional trips to Stillwater, St. Paul and Fort Snelling. Owned and operated by Capt. Charles Barger, clerks A. Papin and Monroeville Greene and others, she was in the St. Louis wharf fire May 1849 and burned along with 22 more boats.

Regulator *1851–1862, sternwheel 155 tons.* Built at Shousetown PA: 155x24.5x4.5'. She first ran as a low-water packet on the upper Ohio R. and was sold to the St. Louis & Keokuk Packet Co.—John McKee ran her below Keokuk between the rapids for a time. She also ran on the Illinois and made at least one trip through to St. Paul in 1852. In 1855 she was a regular St. Paul–St. Louis packet and was on the Missouri R. in 1856. A powerful and fast boat, she was bought by Capt. `Obe' Eames in 1857, who ran her as a towboat out of Stillwater

until 1861. She sank at the Prescott levee in 1860 but apparently was refloated. Dismantled at Wacouta, her machinery went into the *Clara Eames* in 1862.

Relief *1838–1842, sidewheel 78 tons.* Built at Cincinnati by the Harris brothers of Galena as a low-water boat to operate with *Smelter*, hence the name. She was advertised in 1838 for the Upper Mississippi and Rock rivers. Capt. Durant says she came up the St. Croix but there is no other evidence she came above Galena. Off the lists 1842.

Revenue Cutter *1844–1851, sternwheel 100 tons.* Built at Pittsburgh: 127x20x4.1'. Joseph Throckmorton bought her to replace a prior boat, *Cora*, that was sold to the Missouri R. She started as a tramp trader on the Ohio R.; by 1847 was in the St. Louis–Galena trade, owners Capt. McMahan and Oliver Harris; later ran Galena–St. Peters, McMahan master. In 1847 she was engaged to tow a raft through Lake St. Croix for the St. Croix Mill Co. She carried 150 soldiers to Fort Snelling in 1848, made four trips up the Des Moines R. in 1849, once as far as Eddyville with the Keosauqua Democratic Brass Band aboard. She was sometimes called "Rope Cutter" for the habit her officers had of cutting the ropes on ferryboats that got in her way. Off lists 1851.

Robert Fulton *1845–1851, sidewheel 199 tons.* Built at Pittsburgh and named for the steamboat's inventor. This boat ran on the Red R. of the south in 1847, but was noted at Muscatine IA in 1850 and at St. Paul in 1851 as a transient trader. Snagged and lost at Bainbridge MO December 1851.

Rock River *1841–1847, sternwheel 49 tons.* 98'9"x16'3"x3'3"; flush deck. Built on Rock River and originally named *N. P. Hawks,* this small sternwheeler did business on that river until a half interest was purchased by Hungarian expatriate, Agoston Haraszthy. Haraszthy renamed her *Rock River* and ran her on the Wisconsin and Mississippi. She was the first unchartered packet to operate north of Galena. In late 1841 she ferried boards from the St. Croix to finish the chapel of St. Paul. She made 3 trips to the St. Peters/St. Croix in 1843, and for a time she did all the packet business. But with limited boiler surface and green wood to burn, she lacked power and "was frequently excelled in speed by Indians and hunters in their canoes." When she was frozen in at Wacouta, head of Lake Pepin, in the winter of 1844, the cook and other employees walked out on the ice to La Crosse. Haraszthy sold her next spring to New Orleans, where she was better able cope with the current of the bayous. Off lists 1847.

Rolla *1837–1838, sidewheel 139 tons.* Built at Pittsburgh: single engine. From the port of Pittsburgh she was chartered by the War Department to take the Dakota back to their homes after the treaty making in Washington in the summer of 1837. That November a flue collapsed and she caught fire at Rock Island, killing a fireman and severely injuring the engineer. She survived the incident, however, finally sinking October 1838.

Rosalie *1839–1842, sidewheel 145 tons.* Built at Pittsburgh. She was in the St. Louis–Galena trade in 1839, Capt. M. Littleton, when she was advertised in Galena for a pleasure trip to the St. Peters. Off lists 1842.

Royal Arch *1852–1858, sidewheel 212 tons.* Built at West Elizabeth PA: 171x26'6"x4'4". She was sunk on the Ohio R. in her maiden year, re-outfitted and sold to the Galena & Minnesota Packet Co. In 1854 they brought her into the daily packet line where she ran for the 1854–6 seasons, Capt. E. H. Gleim. Described then as a "roomy boat, nearly new," she became very popular with the traveling public. She was noted at Stillwater April and June 1854 en route to St. Paul. Later, along with the *Greek Slave,* she handled reshipping from the Rock Island Railroad (which had just opened) to Dubuque. Capt. J. J. Smith was master in 1858 when she was snagged and lost at Nine Mile Island below Dubuque.

Rufus Putnam *1822–1826, sidewheel 68 tons.* Built at Marietta OH. She was a small boat that boasted high-pressure engines and ran on the Muskingum R. 1–2 years before being bought by Capt. David C. Bates in spring of 1825. The *Putnam* took supplies to Fort Snelling in April 1825, and returned in May with trade goods for the Columbia Fur Co. post at Land's End (Bloomington MN). This is the first steamboat known to have carried traders supplies as well as first to go any distance on the Minnesota R., although she ascended only a mile. Bates ran her in the Upper Mississippi trade until 1826, when she was snagged.

S

Saint Anthony *1846–1851, sidewheel 184 tons.* Built at Belle Vernon PA: 157x24x5'; engines 22", 7' stroke, three boilers; light tuck, no gallery. This small but highly furnished sidewheel packet boasted 30 staterooms. Capt. A. G. Montford ran her in the Galena–St. Peters regular trade in 1846 and on the St. Croix. That summer she was used to move troops from the Upper Mississippi to the Mexican War. In July 1846 she struck a rock during low water and sank. When raised she went to the Pittsburgh trade. Burned opposite St. Charles MO 1851.

Saint Croix *1844–1867, sidewheel 158 tons.* Built at St. Louis by Hiram Bersie, William Cupps, James Ryan and James Ward, who ran her. Capt. Bersie had her in the St. Louis–Galena–St. Peters trade 1845–7 with stops at Stillwater (James Ward, later president of the Northern Line, was mate). A trim and speedy craft, in 1845 she raced Smith Harris's *War Eagle* (1) from St. Louis to Galena, but gave up when the Harris boat set a new record of 43 hours and 52 minutes. After being in collision with *Mermaid* at Quincy in April 1845, losing her barge, and being damaged by fire that May, she had a long and successful life, going to the wreckers June 1867 at St. Louis.

Saint Louis & Galena Packet *1826-?, 150 tons, rig unknown.* Built at New Albany IN. Through 1827–29 St. Louis and Galena papers mention the "St. Louis and Galena Packet," or "Galena Packet," or occasionally just "the Packet," which is noted for towing one of the earliest safety barges, *Lady Washington.* In 1827 Capt. S. Shallcross had her in the Galena lead trade with the barge, which drew only 11″ giving her immense capacity. In April 1828 he attempted to ascend the Wisconsin R. with lead to be shipped via the Fox R. but made only a few miles before having to turn back. In 1829 Capt. John Shallcross is recorded at St. Louis loading the *Lady Washington* for Fort Snelling, but it is not clear if this refers to the barge or to a

steamboat active at that time. No packet is recorded under the name *Saint Louis & Galena Packet*, and the boat referred to may have been the steamboat *Lady Washington* (which see).

Saint Louis Oak *1842–1848, sidewheel 108 tons.* Built at St. Louis. This packet usually ran St. Louis–Galena–Dubuque, but was logged at least once at Stillwater, Capt. James I. Dorier in command. Snagged on the Missouri R. in 1847, but noted there again in 1848, Capt. Abram Shinkle. Off records 1848.

Saint Paul *1852–1857, sidewheel 226 tons.* Built at Wheeling VA: 108x24x4′6″, engines 18's, 6′ stroke. Built by the Harris brothers of Galena for the lower river, she was first registered in April 1852. She was lengthened considerably prior to 1854 and reentered the trade as *New Saint Paul*, by which name she is better known (see *New Saint Paul*).

Saint Peters 1 *1835–1838, sidewheel 119 tons.* Built at Pittsburgh: single engine. Owned by Capt. Joseph Throckmorton and the firm of Hempstead & Beebe of St. Louis, she was purchased by principals of the American Fur Co. for the fur trade. She arrived at Fort Snelling Jul. 2, 1836, with geographer Joseph N. Nicollet and 30 St. Louis excursionists on their way to the Falls of St. Anthony. Throckmorton was master through the fall of 1836, when he went to Pittsburgh to build *Ariel* and *Burlington.* Capt. Chouteau had her on the Missouri R.; when at Fort Clark ND in 1837 she brought smallpox to the upper Indian tribes, which killed a great number of them. Dismantled 1838.

Saint Peters 2 *1844–1849, sidewheel 163 tons.* Built at St. Louis. Part-owner James Ward, formerly mate of the *Saint Croix,* was on her from the start, and master 1848–9 in the St. Louis–Galena–Dubuque-Potosi lead trade. She burned in the St. Louis fire of May 1849; loss $3,000 ($70,000).

Sangamon   *1853–1856, sidewheel 85 tons.* Built at New Albany IN. A little sidewheel steamer, she was noted as a fast traveler. She made at least one trip to St. Paul in 1854, Capt. R. M. Spencer, and entered the Minnesota R. trade that year. She was able to get up the river above Mankato in May 1854, hauling supplies to Fort Ridgely. Snagged and lost at St. Charles AR, February 1856.

Sarah Ann   *1841–1845, sidewheel 162 tons.* Built at Pittsburgh. Her home port was St. Louis, but she advertised a tour to the St. Peters in 1841, and also appeared on the St. Croix that summer, Capt. Lafferty. She was sunk and raised in 1841. Off lists 1845.

Science   *1834–1838, sidewheel 52 tons.* Built at Fredericktown PA. Although her first port was Pittsburgh, during the 1837 season Capt. Clark made regular trips from St. Louis and Galena to Helena WI (on the Wisconsin R.) with two runs to Fort Winnebago at Portage. She probably did not come above Prairie du Chien. Off lists 1838.

Scioto   *1823–1826, sidewheel 170 tons.* Built at Gallipolis OH: single engine. She started as a lower river boat, but was hired by the army to deliver supplies to Fort Snelling, arriving in May 1826 with passengers and goods for the Indian agent. She left for Prairie du Chien May 27 to bring up the balance of the public stores and returned June 1 having made the round trip in 6 days. Her master was S. K. Gillchrest. Off lists 1827.

Senator   *1846–1852, sidewheel 121 tons.* Built at Wheeling VA and sometimes called *U. S. Senator.* This low-water Upper Mississippi boat was first spring arrival at Galena from St. Louis in 1847 and was on the St. Croix that year, Capt. E. M. McCoy. In 1848 Smith Harris bought her to oppose the Galena & Minnesota Packet Co., selling her to the company in 1849 at a handsome profit. In 1849 she was hired to transport the Winnebago to their new Minnesota reservation. An exceptionally slow boat, she lost much trade to the fickle public. Orrin Smith was master 1849–50. Off lists 1852.

Shenandoah   *1848–1856, sidewheel 179 tons.* Built at Brownsville PA. In October 1849, while in the Ohio R.–St. Louis trade, she knocked down her stacks passing the Louisville Canal drawbridge. As replacement for the *Dr. Franklin No. 2,* which burned at St. Louis, she made 5 trips from St. Louis to St. Paul in 1853 under Capt. Eugene Leveille. She was still in that trade in 1855. In 1853 (a high-water year) she made 3 trips up the Minnesota R. as well, on one trip losing her guards off the ladies' cabin at one bend. Destroyed by ice (and collision of floating boats) at St. Louis Feb. 27, 1856.

Smelter   *1837–1843, sidewheel 180 tons.* Built at Cincinnati by Smith and Scribe Harris, she was described as the fastest, most luxurious and largest boat on the Upper Mississippi. She was one of the first tourist boats and the first on the upper river with private staterooms. Exceptionally proud of their speedy boat, the Harrises decorated her with evergreens and mounted a cannon on her prow that was fired when rounding to at landings or meeting other boats. In 1837 she was a Galena–St. Peters packet and also made the "fashionable tour" to the Falls of St. Anthony. That year she set the Galena–Cincinnati speed record: 5 days. Off lists 1843.

Stella Blanche *1853–1855, sidewheel 202 tons.* Built at Paducah KY. She began operating on the Ohio, but in 1854 switched to the Upper Mississippi, making several trips. She was noted that June at St. Louis from Dubuque with meat, wheat, barley, oats, and potatoes. Off lists 1855.

T

Tempest *1846–1854, sidewheel 210 tons.* Built at St. Louis: 175x25x5′. She operated out of St. Louis as the regular St. Louis, Galena, Dubuque and Potosi packet and was logged at Galena Apr. 11, 1846, Capt. John Smith. That spring she brought Galena news of the Mexican War. She collided with *Talisman* in 1847 near Cape Girardeau, was repaired and ran Alton–St. Louis in 1849. Off lists 1854.

Tennessee *1836–1843, sidewheel 86 tons.* Built at Bridgeport PA. Usually a Pittsburgh–St. Louis steamer, in April 1841 she was chartered by the St. Croix Lumber Co. to bring up supplies and machinery for the new sawmill at St. Croix Falls. Most of the principals were on board also, having spent the winter in St. Louis. Off lists 1843.

Tiger *1849–1853, screw propeller 83 tons.* Built at Sauk City WI on the Wisconsin R.: 100x18′. She had the engines from *Otter*, which was sunk at Sauk City, but they put out only 52 hp. She was often ragged about her lack of speed—one wag said she had "lost a race with a sawmill." In 1850 Capt. O. H. Maxwell had her at St. Paul and on the St.

Croix; she was at St. Paul from Dubuque, Capt. Anderson, 6 times in 1851. Capt. Barton also ran her on the Minnesota R. in 1852–3, carrying settlers to the new town of Mankato. In July 1853 she departed St. Paul with supplies for the new Fort Ridgely—in all Capt. Ruby made 13 trips with her that year, many above Mankato. Her rig is a mystery: one source calls her a sidewheeler, but others agree she was propeller-driven. She disappeared in late 1853.

Time & Tide 1 *1845–1847, sidewheel 119 tons.* Built at Louisville KY. Smith Harris ran her for part of the 1845 season while his brother Scribe and A. G. Montford commanded *Lightfoot*. That June the two boats brought excursionists to Fort Snelling. They left Galena with their bows lashed together—*Time* serving as promenade and dance salon, *Lightfoot* as dining hall and hotel. She was also on the St. Croix that fall under Capt. Charles Barger. In 1846 her captain was William Hooper and she was in the St. Louis–Galena trade. Snagged and sunk October 1847.

Time & Tide 2 *1847–1853, sidewheel 161 tons.* Built at Louisville KY. This regular St. Louis–Galena–St. Peters packet was owned and run by Capt. E. W. Gould of St. Louis. Sold 1848 to the Naples Packet Co., she ran with the *Anthony Wayne* in regular service on the Illinois R. connecting with Gould & Rodgers' new rail line. She was back on the upper river in 1849, stopping at Stillwater. Stranded and lost at St. Louis March 1853.

Time & Tide 3 *1853–1864, sidewheel 130 tons.* Built at Freedom PA: 128x26.7x4.1′. Capt. E. W. Gould and other St. Louis businessmen built her to replace the *Time & Tide* (2). She was at St. Paul,

Capt. Louis Robert, 1855–6; on the Minnesota R., same master, 1857–8 and Capt. Nelson Robert 1859–60. Capt. Robert liked to joke that his boat would wait for no man, but would wait 15 minutes for one woman. She was sold in 1861 to New Orleans, where she was rebuilt in 1862, and burned in 1864.

U

Uncle Toby *1844–1853, sidewheel 109 tons.* Built at Pittsburgh. An Upper Mississippi workhorse, she was noted at the St. Peters from St. Louis, Capt. George B. Cole, in 1845; was a regular St. Louis–Galena–Dubuque–Prairie du Chien packet 1846; and ran St. Louis to St. Peters in 1847–1851, Capt. Henry R. Day. In October 1851 she ascended the Minnesota R. with the first load of Indian annuity goods under the new treaty. Her lack of speed ascending the St. Croix was noted by a sleepless traveler, "From the first we heard the boat down the river until it went by and was unheard in the distance above, was a lapse of nearly half the night." She arrived at Point Douglas in late November 1851 and because of floating ice off-loaded and teamed the freight to St. Paul, then returned to St. Louis. Off lists 1853.

V

Valley Forge *1839–1845, sidewheel 199 tons.* Built at Pittsburgh: 150x25x5.5′; iron hull, 4 boilers. She had good power and was the first iron-hulled steamboat on the Ohio and Mississippi rivers. In 1839–40 Capts. Isaac Hooper and Thomas Baldwin used her for tours on the Ohio R. In 1840 she was advertised for an excursion from Pittsburgh to the "the Indian Country and Falls of St. Anthony." Off lists 1845.

Versailles *1831–1835, sidewheel 83 tons.* Built at Cincinnati. She was the first boat up to Fort Snelling in May 1832, carrying the only supplies the post had seen since the preceding November. Snagged and lost January 1835 at Apalachicola FL.

Vienna *1852?–1857, sternwheel 169 tons.* Built at Monongahela PA. Although listed as built in 1853, this sternwheeler must have been registered earlier, as she appeared at St. Paul in November of 1852, one of the last boats up. Her owners were brothers George B. and Charles A. Hay who put her into the regular St. Louis–Stillwater–St. Paul trade 1855–6, Charles C. Hay, master. Lost in the ice on the Illinois R. February 1857.

Virginia *1819–1823?, sidewheel 109 tons.* Built at Wheeling VA: 118x18′10″x5′2″. She was at St. Louis in May 1821 commanded by Capt. Pemberton with a "company on board pleased with their passage from Wheeling." Shallcross was her master when she was noted loading government stores in St. Louis April 23, 1823. That spring she was the first steamboat to reach Fort Snelling, arriving May 10, 1823, under Capt. John Crawford. After running the long Des Moines rapids at Keokuk and the upper rapids at Rock Island, she was 729 miles from St. Louis. On board were army paymaster Maj. Thomas Biddle, Lt. Joseph Russell, Indian agent Lawrence Taliaferro, and an Italian explorer, Giacomo Beltrami. *Virginia* didn't look much like later river steamboats. She had a small cabin aft on her single deck, had no pilot house, and was guided by a tiller at the stern. Some think she carried a sail, but her

1822 registration shows her mastless. Snagged and supposedly lost at Chester IL Sep. 19, 1823, she may have been refloated as a *Virginia* is again mentioned at St. Louis in 1825–6.

Volant   *dates, rig and tonnage unknown.* This government supply boat arrived at Fort Snelling sometime before May 1826. This boat is still unidentified. Although there were many steamboats of this name active in the 1830s, none of them seem to have been built this early.

W

Walk in the Water   *1850–1855, sidewheel 118 tons.* Built in New Albany IN, she at first operated out of Louisville. By 1854 she was in the St. Louis–Dubuque trade. Her name commemorates one of the first Great Lakes steamboats of 1820. Off lists 1855.

War Eagle 1   *1845–1851, sidewheel 155 tons.* Built at Cincinnati: 152x24x4.5′. She was built for Capt. Daniel Smith Harris who commanded her in the Galena–St. Peters trade through 1847, and ran her St. Louis–St. Peters in 1848. A luxury boat and very fast, she broke all records in quick succession, was described as the "swiftest boat of her size on the western waters." Nonetheless, Harris sold her in 1848 to buy *Senator*, an even faster boat. She was at Stillwater in 1845–7, served as a Mexican War troop ship in 1846, and in 1847 took the first known raft tow through Lake Pepin. She appeared on the Missouri R. under Capt. Nick Wall in 1848. Dismantled for use as a barge in 1851.

War Eagle 2   *1854–1870, sidewheel 296 tons.* Built at Fulton OH: 225x27′, 3 boilers. She was built for the Galena & Minnesota Packet Co. at a cost of $33,000 ($700,000 today) to run Galena to St. Paul. She was on the St. Croix and Minnesota rivers that year captained by Smith Harris of Galena. She was excellently furnished with velvet carpet, gilt-framed mirrors and oil paintings as befit the lead boat in the 1854 Grand Excursion. Sold to W. F. Davidson's La Crosse Packet Line in 1859, then to the U.S. service in 1862 during which she took a shot in one of her stacks. In 1870 she burned to the waterline at La Crosse with loss of two lives and $213,000 (nearly $3 million) in property damage. Her roof bell is on a school in Bellevue IA. In 1985, the wreck site in the Black R. was determined to be eligible for the National Register of Historic Places.

Warrior 1   *1826–1829, sidewheel 95 tons.* Built at Marietta OH. Chartered by the army to carry supplies to Fort Snelling, she made at least one trip before May 1826. She collided with *Erie* in January 1829 near Jackson AL and was lost.

Warrior 2   *1832–1837, sidewheel 100 tons.* Built at Pittsburgh: 111′5″x19′x5′, 3 boilers. Owned by Joseph Throckmorton and William Hempstead of Galena, she was a serviceable boat with one deck, a transom stern, a cabin above-deck for officers and crew and a figurehead. As she had no passenger cabin, she was one of the few upper river boats to tow a safety barge for excursionists. She was pressed into service in the 1832 Black Hawk War and ordered to patrol the Mississippi; a small 6-pounder was placed on her bow which she used to halt the Indians' advance near De Soto WI. She first arrived at Fort Snelling in May 1834 carrying Gideon and Samuel Pond to their new mission at Lake Harriet. In June 1835 she was back with Iowa Gov. George W. Jones, painter George Catlin and other notables, and she made two more trips that season. Capt. E. H. Gleim had her in the upper river trade 1836. Snagged 1837.

West Newton *1849–1853, sidewheel 163 tons.* Built at Elizabeth PA. Smith Harris bought her in 1852 at a cost of $25,000 (figure $580,000 today) to beat the *Nominee.* Both boats made 2 trips a week Galena to St. Paul. The intense competition led to consolidation of the two packet companies over the winter of 1852–53; Smith Harris was made a director of the Galena & Minnesota Packet Co. *West Newton* was at Stillwater many times 1852–3 and at the St. Paul levee 27 times in 1853. On Apr. 27, 1853, she carried two companies of the 6th U. S. Regiment to newly built Fort Ridgely, having two barges with the baggage in tow. She was noted for a race with the *Die Vernon* Jul. 13–14, 1853—she lost the race but won fame. She was snagged and lost at Alma WI October 1853 at a location later called West Newton Chute, where she stayed, a terror to navigation, until dynamited in August 1910. *West Newton* is the only Upper Mississippi boat known to have two villages (both now gone) named for her: West Newton in West Newton Township, Nicollet Co., MN on the Minnesota R. and West Newton, Wabasha Co., MN on the Mississippi near where she was wrecked–her name-board is said to have marked the latter village.

Winnebago *1830–1836, sidewheel 91 tons.* Built at Pittsburgh. Capt. Joseph Throckmorton bought *Winnebago* in 1831 and formed a combination with James May of the *Enterprise* (2). He sold his interest

the same year and went to built *Warrior* (2) in the winter of 1831–2. In 1832 Lt. Jefferson Davis took the defeated Sauk chief Black Hawk and 11 of his warriors to Jefferson Barracks MO on her. Her master then was Capt. Phil K. Hunt. Off Registration list 1836.

Wisconsin *1834–1838?, sidewheel 87 tons.* Built at Pittsburgh. This small packet appeared in the Galena trade in 1834. She is noted arriving at Galena in 1835, Capt. Henry Crossle, with two keelboats heavily laden with freight and passengers. She was in regular service from Galena and Dubuque to Prairie du Chien in 1836, Capt. O'Flaherty. Collided with *Tiskilwa* in the Illinois R. and sunk March 1837, but later raised, as she is noted arriving in St. Louis from Fort Winnebago at the portage on the Wisconsin R. in May of 1838. Final disposition unknown.

Wyoming *1846–1853, sidewheel 198 tons.* Built at Jacksonville PA. Capt. William J. Kountz bought her 1847 and she was later on the Upper Mississippi. She carried freight from Moline IL and Galena to Stillwater and St. Paul in 1851. Burned at Pekin IL December 1853.

Y

Yankee *1847–1852, sternwheel 97 tons.* Built at Glasgow PA: 145′ long. She was on the Ohio in 1849, but that September made a trip to St. Paul. In July 1850 Capt. Keeler Harris took this ambitious little boat with a party of St. Paul notables and the Fort Snelling military band up the Minnesota R. past Mankato, besting previous records. She made several trips to Stillwater in 1850, operated at

St. Paul in 1851, Capt. Orrin Smith. Next season she was sold to run on the Cedar (IA) R. Off lists 1852.

Yellow Stone *1831–1837, sidewheel 144 tons.* Built at Louisville KY: 120x20x6'. Built by Pierre Chouteau Jr. of St. Louis for service in the Missouri R. fur trade, on her first trip under Capt. Andrew G. Bennett she ascended 600 miles further than any boat before. In 1832 she carried painter George Catlin to the mouth of the Yellowstone R. and in 1833 Prince Maximilian came up the Missouri on her. She went to the Mississippi lead trade in 1834, running St. Louis to Galena. That year she also was chartered to carry the old Sac war chief Black Hawk to Prairie du Chien. She was sold to New Orleans in 1835. Her final disposition is unknown, although she is popularly believed to have been stranded and lost on the Brazos R. in 1837. She disappears after that year.

York State *1852–1859, sidewheel 247 tons.* Built at Brownsville PA for the St. Louis & Keokuk Packet Co., she ran as a weekly St. Louis–Galena mail packet under Capt. Thomas H. Griffiths. She was running St. Louis to St. Paul in 1854–5 (although only one source attests to the 1854 date). Capt. James Ward bought her in the fall of 1855. She was snagged and lost on the Illinois R. 1859.

Glossary of Steamboating Terms

American Fur Co. — this term is used throughout to refer to a fur trading firm that operated under several names over the years. The western division, headquartered in St. Louis, became Pratte, Chouteau & Co. in 1834 and Pierre Chouteau, Jr. & Co. in 1838. The eastern division, headquartered at Mackinac Is., sold out to Pierre Chouteau Jr. & Co. in 1842. Both branches were colloquially referred to as the American Fur Co. even after that firm ceased to exist.

annuity boat — a boat hired by the U. S. government to carry yearly supplies to Indian bands as specified in their treaties.

barge — a flat-bottomed, unpowered boat.

bateau — a flat bottomed rowboat pointed at both ends (plural bateaux).

boatyard — place where boats are built.

boiler deck — the second deck of a steamboat on which the cabin is built, forming a roof for the main deck.

bow — the front of a boat.

broadhorn — a flatboat or barge, steered by oars.

buckets — the wooden paddles of a paddlewheel.

bull railings — removable wood railings that fit between the stanchions on the main deck to contain cargo or animals.

bushwhacking — moving a boat upstream by pulling on bushes or branches.

cabin — an enclosed room on any deck.

cabin crew — staff that serves the main cabin passengers; a large boat might carry stewards, cooks, cabin boys, chambermaids and waiters.

captain — the officer in charge of a boat, also called master, commander.

capstan — a cylinder on the forward part of the main deck used as a winch.

charter — a boat hired for a specific trip.

chimney — smokestack.

chute — a narrows or fast-flowing rapids.

clerk — the boat's business officer.

cordelling — moving a boat upstream by pulling on a rope tied to the boat's mast.

cub — an apprentice crewman, as a cub pilot.

Dakota or Sioux — Indians who lived in northern Iowa and southern Minnesota.

deckhand — crewman on a steamboat, also called roustabout.

Des Moines rapids — the lower rapids, at the mouth of the Des Moines River (Keokuk).

draft — the depth a boat sinks into the water; draft is given as light (unloaded) and loaded.

engineer — the person in charge of the boiler and engines of a steamboat.

escape pipe — a pipe in the main steam line to let off excess steam.

firebox — the compartment in which wood is burned to heat water in the boilers.

fireman — crew member who stokes the fires under the boiler.

flatboat — also called ark, barge or broadhorn; a rectangular, flat-bottomed unpowered boat.

flue — a duct conveying heat from the firebox to the boiler.

Fort Armstrong — U.S. army fort at Rock Island IL, construction started 1816.

Fort Crawford — U.S. army fort at Prairie du Chien WI, built 1816 on site of Fort Shelby.

Fort Snelling — U.S. army fort at the junction of the Minnesota and Mississippi rivers (Minneapolis) built 1820–6.

forwarding agent — (or commission agent) firm that takes freight from a steamboat, stores it and reships it to the ultimate destination.

fur company — a company in the business of trading goods to the Indians for furs and hides; when capitalized, the American Fur Company.

galena — lead ore, the mining of which gave Galena, Illinois, its name.

gangplank — a plank that extends from main deck to shore to permit loading.

gingerbread trim — fancy woodwork or fretwork on the upper decks of a steamboat.

grasshoppering — a method of jacking up the front of a steamboat to dislodge it from a sandbar, sometimes called sparring.

guards — extensions of the main deck beyond the hull that protect the sidewheels and allow extra cargo space and a walkway.

gunboat — slang term for a floating house of prostitution.

high-pressure engine — a powerful engine developed specifically for steamboats that used high-pressure steam and a small cylinder.

hog chains — an external system of bracing for the hull of a steamboat.

hogging — the tendency of a steamboat hull to arch in the middle because of the weight at both ends.

hold — the cargo space beneath the main deck, enclosed by the hull.

hull — the boat's bottom.

hurricane deck — the roof of the main cabin and staterooms, also called hurricane roof.

jackstaff — flagpost mounted on the bow of a boat.

keel — a timber extending along the bottom of a vessel to give stability; riverboats were built without keels.

keelboat — a boat built on a keel with covered cargo area, which could be propelled upstream by sailing, poling, cordelling, warping or rowing.

keelson — framing timber in lieu of a keel on the floor of a steamboat's hull.

Lake Pepin — the widening of the Mississippi above the Chippewa River bar.

Lake St. Croix — the widening of the St. Croix River above its mouth from Prescott WI to Stillwater MN.

landing stage — a suspended gangplank that can be swung out from the boat to the shore.

lay by — to hold a boat stationary; to dock.

lead district — the mining area around Galena IL, Mineral Point, Platteville and Potosi WI and Dubuque IA.

let go — to untie the lines, cast off.

levee — boat landing at a city.

light — an unloaded boat; a boat's draft is usually given light.

lighter — a small boat used to temporarily take cargo off a steamboat to enable it to pass a shallow spot.

lighting — the practice of off-loading cargo onto a flatboat or other lighter.

line — any rope, cable or pipe.

line service — several boats providing regular service in a given trade; the boats might be owned separately or in common, with each partner owning a fraction of all boats.

Little Rapids — two slight falls in the Minnesota River near Carver, MN that in low water prevented passage of larger steamboats from going further.

low-pressure engine — early steamboat engine based on stationary engines, with a large cylinder and low steam pressure.

lower rapids — also called Des Moines rapids; the rapids at Keokuk which sometimes were a bar to navigation for larger boats.

Lower Mississippi — the Mississippi River from New Orleans to St. Louis.

main cabin — the passenger cabin, usually located on the boiler deck.

main deck — the deck on which the boilers sit.

make fast — to tie a boat up.

mate — officer in charge of the deckhands and loading of the steamboat.

mud clerk — the junior clerk, whose responsibilities often included standing in the mud while cargo was off-loaded.

mud drum — a cylinder beneath the boilers that collects sediment.

Ojibwe or Chippewa — Indians who lived in central to northern Wisconsin and Minnesota.

Otoe — Indians who lived in western Iowa, Nebraska and South Dakota.

packet — steamboat that is available to haul passengers and freight.

packet company — (or packet line) company formed by several steamboat owners to provide scheduled service in a trade.

paddle boxes — the protective cover for the side paddlewheels.

paddlewheel — a wheel fitted with buckets, or paddles, that propels the boat.

panorama — twelve-foot wide canvas hundreds of feet long painted with scenes that were unrolled before the viewer to recreate a trip on the river.

pilot — steersman for a raft or boat.

pilothouse — the nerve center of a steamboat, the pilot's cabin with the steering wheel.

pineries — pine forests of northern Wisconsin and Minnesota where lumber camps were located.

pitman — the long connecting rod between piston and crank on a steamboat engine.

ply, to — to work steadily, usually between two stated points.

poling — to propel a boat by poles set in the river bottom.

raftboat — (or rafter) a towboat powerful enough to control a log raft in the river's current.

railhead — the terminal of a railroad line.

railroad ferry — a steamboat that transfers rail cars across a river.

Rock Island rapids — the upper rapids of the
Mississippi River extending above Rock Is.

rosin — a highly flammable turpentine product,
used to aid combustion.

run, a — the usual course of a boat as it moves
freight and/or passengers.

safety barge — a barge fitted out to carry passengers, towed by a steamboat; the passengers
ride in comfort away from the boiler and
engines.

safety valve — a relief valve that opens when boiler
steam pressure becomes excessive.

St. Peters, the — area around the junction of the
Minnesota and Mississippi rivers, including
Fort Snelling, Mendota and St. Anthony
Falls.

St. Peters River — old name for the Minnesota
River, changed in 1852.

salon, saloon — (the words had the same meaning
in 1854) the main cabin on a steamboat.

sandbar — sand deposit close to or at the surface.

Sac and Fox — (also Mesquakie) Indians who lived
in western Illinois and eastern Iowa. Sac is
often written Sauk.

sheer — the marked rise in a boat's main deck at
bow and stern.

shoal — shallows or water with little depth, an
underwater sandbar.

showboat — usually a barge fitted out with a
theater moved by a towboat; sometimes self-
propelled.

sidewheeler — a steamboat propelled by two
centrally mounted paddlewheels.

skylight roof — a roof protruding through the
hurricane deck with skylights to let light into
the main cabin.

snag — an obstruction in the river, usually dead
wood such as logs and stumps; to run a boat
upon a snag, putting a hole in her hull.

stage — same as a landing stage.

stanchions — vertical framing posts that support a
deck, also called stationaries.

staterooms — individual bedrooms opening off the
main cabin and also outside onto the boiler
deck.

steering oar — a long pole with a plank on the end
used to steer a flatboat or raft.

steersman — a hand who operates the wheel in the
pilot house directed by the pilot.

stern — the rear of a boat.

sternwheel — paddlewheel boat with a single
paddlewheel at the rear.

steward — officer of the second class, in charge of
the passengers' comfort and meals.

stick — slang for to run aground.

striker — apprentice crewman, especially to the
engineer; also called cub.

texas — cabin on the skylight roof, usually reserved
for the officers.

tons, tonnage — the carrying capacity of a steamboat, one ton equaling 100 cubic feet; gross
tonnage is the boat's total capacity; net
tonnage is calculated by subtracting space
taken up by the boat's machinery and crew's
quarters.

tow — another vessel, raft or barge pushed, or
sometimes hauled, by a steamboat.

towboat — a boat that pushes, or tows, a barge or
keelboat.

trade — the area of operation of a steamboat, usually stated as between two ports.

tramp — a free-lance steamboat roaming from trade to trade.

transient — same as a tramp; also sometimes called a `wild´ boat.

transom — the vertical part of the stern of a boat; also a small hinged window to let light into the main cabin.

treaties of 1837 — treaties with the Ojibwe and Dakota that opened up land in Wisconsin and Minnesota east of the Mississippi to settlement.

treaties of 1851 — treaties with the Dakota that opened up southern Minnesota to settlement.

upper rapids — also called Rock Island rapids; the rapids of the Mississippi extending above Rock Island.

Upper Mississippi — the river above St. Louis; in the context of this book, the river above Galena, IL.

warping — moving a boat upstream by taking a rope ahead, tying it to a tree (or tree buried in a sandbar) and winching the boat up to it.

Winnebago — (also Hochunk) Indians who lived in south central Wisconsin.

wharfboat — the hulk of a steamboat moored to provide a place for boats to tie up to.

wheelhouse — protective casing around the side paddlewheel

wood boat — a flatboat loaded with firewood taken in tow until emptied, then let loose to float back.

wood yard — a place along the river stockpiling fuel for steamboats.

wooding — taking on fuel, from a wood yard or by sending parties ashore to cut timber.

wood up, to — slang term for wooding a steamboat.

Bibliography

Newspapers and Periodicals

Burlington IA *Saturday Evening Post* 1915-26
Burlington IA *Patriot* 1839-41
Chicago *Daily Tribune* June 5-13, 1854
Cleveland *Herald* June 9, 1954
Davenport IA *The Half-Century Democrat* Oct. 22, 1905
Davenport IA *Iowa Democratic Enquirer* 1849-50
Dubuque UA *Visitor* 1836
Dubuque IA *Weekly Tribune* 1852-53
Galena Northwestern *Gazette and Galena Advertiser* 1828-54
Galena IL City Directories 1838-
Galena *Jeffersonian* 1846-54
Galena *Northwest Gazette and Galena Advertiser* 1840-2
Louisville KY *Louisville Journal*, May 21, 1844
Madison WI *Express* Jan. 2, June 2, July 28, 1841
Minneapolis *Sunday Tribune* Nov. 15, 1934
New Haven CT *Palladium* 1854
New York Times June 20, 1854
Prairie du Chien WI *Crawford County Courier* 1852
St. Louis *Daily Democrat* 1853-54
St. Louis *Missouri Angus* 1838-39
St. Louis *Missouri Republican* 1833
St. Paul *Dispatch* 12-14-1980, 5-14-1982
St. Paul *Minnesota Pioneer* 1849-54
St. Paul *Pioneer & Democrat* 1854
St. Paul *Weekly Minnesotian* 1852-54
St. Paul *Daily Minnesotian* 1854
Stillwater *Messenger* 1856-57
Stillwater *St. Croix Union* 1854-55
Taylors Falls *Dalles Visitor* summer 1974 and 1984
Winona *Daily News* (heritage edition 10-31-1986)

Books and Articles

Ahlgren, Dorothy Eaton and Mary Cotter Beeler, *History of Prescott, Wisconsin* (1996)
Andrews, James A., "Early Times in St. Croix County," *Wisconsin Magazine of History* 14/7 (December 1930)
Baker, James H., "History of Transportation in Minnesota," *Minn. Hist. Collections* IX (1901)
Bell, Edwin, "Early Steamboating on the Minnesota and Red Rivers," *Minnesota Historical Collections* X/i (1905)
Blair, Walter, *A Raft Pilot's Log ... 1840-1915* (1930)
Blakeley, Russell, "History . . . of Commerce in Minnesota," *Minn. Hist. Colls.* VIII (1898)
Blegen, Theodore C., "The `Fashionable Tour' on the Upper Mississippi," *Minnesota History* 20/4 (December 1939)
Bliss, John H., "Reminiscences of Fort Snelling," *Minnesota Historical Collections* VI (1894)
Bond, J. W., *Minnesota and Its Resources* (1853)
Buck, Anita A., *Steamboats on the St. Croix* (1990)
Bunnell, Lafayette W., *Winona and Its Environs...* (1897)
Catlin, John, *North American Indians* 2 (1847; 1903 edition)
Dains, Mary K., "Steamboats of the 1850s-1860s: A Pictorial History," *Missouri Historical Revue* 67/2 (1973)
Daniels, Wilson "Steamboating on the Ohio and Mississippi Before the Civil War," *Indiana Magazine of History* 11/2 (June 1915)
Drago, Henry Sinclair, *The Steamboaters* (1967)
Dunn, James Taylor, *Marine on St. Croix: 150 Years of Village Life* (1989)
Dunn, James Taylor, *The St. Croix: Midwest Border River* (reprint 1969)

Durant, Edward W., "Lumbering and Steam-boating on the St. Croix River," *Minnesota Historical Collections* 10/ii (1905)

Easton, Augustus G., *History St. Croix Valley* 2 vols (1909)

Ellet, Elizabeth, *Summer Rambles in the West* (1853)

Eskew, Garnett L., *The Pageant of the Packets: A Book of American Steamboating* (1929)

Farnam, Henry W., *Memoir of Henry Farnam* (1889)

Featherstonhaugh, George W. , *A Canoe Voyage Up the Minnay Sotor,* 1 & 2 (1847; 1970 ed.)

Folsom, William H. C., "History of Lumbering in the St. Croix Valley," *Minnesota Historical Collections* IX (1901)

Folsom, William H. C., *Fifty Years in the Northwest* (1888)

Gould, Emerson W., *Fifty Years on the Mississippi, or Gould's History of River Navigation* (1889)

Hall, James, *The West: Its Commerce and Navigation* (1848)

Halloway, Emory, ed., *The Uncollected Poetry and Prose of Walt Whitman* (1921)

Hartsough, Mildred L., *From Canoe to Steel Barge on the Upper Mississippi* (1934)

Hughes, Thomas, "History of Steamboating on the Minnesota River..." *Minnesota Historical Collections* X/i (1905)

Hunter, Louis C., *Steamboats on the Western Waters: An Economic and Technological History* (1949, 1993 ed.)

Jackson, Donald, *Voyages of the Steamboat Yellow Stone* (1985)

Jakle, John A., *Images of the Ohio Valley* (1977)

Larson, Ron, *Upper Mississippi River History* (1998)

Lass, William E., *History of Steamboating on the Upper Missouri* (1962)

Le Duc, William G., "Minnesota at the Crystal Palace Exhibition, New York, 1853" *Minnesota History Bulletin* I/7 (August 1916)

Lloyd, James T., *Lloyd's Steamboat Directory and Disasters on the Western Waters* (reprint 2000)

Loehr, Rodney C. "William R. Brown Diary 1845-46" in *Minnesota Farmers' Diaries* (1939)

Lytle, William & Forrest Holdcamper, *Merchant Steam Vessels of the United States 1790-1868* (1975)

Mahoney, Timothy R., *River Towns in the Great West* (1990)

Marryat, Frederick, "An English Officer's Description of Wisconsin in 1837," *Wisconsin Historical Collections* XIV (1898)

Marryat, Frederick, *A Diary in America [1838-39]* (1962)

McGinty, Brian, *Strong Wine: The Life and Legend of Agoston Haraszthy* (1998)

Merrick, George B*., Old Times on the Upper Mississippi* (1909)

Merrick, George B. and William Tibbals, *Genesis of Western River Steamboating* (1912)

Mueller, Edward A., *Upper Mississippi Rafting Steamboats*

Morrison, John E., *History of American Steam Navigation* (1967)

Neill, Edward D., "Occurrences In and Around Ft. Snelling from 1819 to 1840," *Minnesota Historical Collections* II (1889)

Oliphant, Laurence, *Minnesota and the Far West* (1855)

Parker, Donald Dean, editor, *The Recollections of Philander Prescott, Frontiersman of the Old Northwest, 1819-1862,* (1966)

Petersen, William J., *Steamboating on the Upper Mississippi* (1937)

Petersen, William J., "Capt. Daniel Smith Harris," *Iowa Journal of History* 28

Petersen, William J., "Captains and Cargoes of Early Upper Mississippi Steamboats," *Wisconsin Magazine of History* 13/3 (March 1930)

Petersen, William J., "Capt. Throckmorton," *Palimpsest* X/4 (April 1929)

Petersen, William J., "The Galena Packet Company," *Iowa Journal of History* 50 (1952)

Petersen, William J., "The Rock Island Excursion of 1854," *Minnesota History* 15/4 (Dec. 1934)

Petersen, W. J., "The Virginia: The `Clermont' of the Upper Mississippi," *Minnesota History* 9/4 (December 1928)

Scharf, John T., *History of St. Louis* (1883)

Sedgwick, Catherine A., "Great Excursion to the Falls of St. Anthony," *Putnams Monthly* 4(1854)

Seymour, Ephraim S., *Sketches of Minnesota, The New England of the West... 1849* (1850)

Smith, William Rudolph, "Journal [1837]," *Wisconsin Magazine of History* 12/3 (March 1929)

Swanholm, Marx and Susan Zeik, "The Tonic of Wildness," *Fort Snelling Chronicles* (1976)

Swanson, Deborah, editor. "Joseph Farr Remembers the Underground Railroad in St. Paul," *Minnesota History* 57/3 (2000)

Toole, Robert C., "Competition and Consolidation: The Galena Packet Company 1848-1863," *Journal of the Ill. State Historical Society* 57 (Fall 1964)

Trowbridge, John Townsend, *The Desolate South, 1865-1868: A Picture of the Battlefields and of the Devastated Confederacy* (1956)

Warner, George and Charles M. Foote, *History of Washington County and the St. Croix Valley* (1881)

Watson, Ken, *Paddle Steamers: An Illustrated History of Steamboats on the Mississippi and Its Tributaries* (1985)

Way, Frederick Jr., *Way's Directory of Western Rivers Packets* (1950 edition)

Way, Frederick Jr., *Way's Packet Directory 1848-1994* (1976, revised by Joseph Rutter 1994)

Winther, Oscar O., *The Transportation Frontier* (1942)

Government documents

St. Louis Harbormasters' Reports and Enrolments, Records of the Bureau of Marine Inspection and Navigation (NARG 41), microfilm, National Archives Regional Office Kansas City

Ship Registers and Enrolments, New Orleans Vols. 1-3, Public Library of Cincinnati and Hamilton County, Cincinnati

Collections

Galena business collection, Galena Public Library

Caleb Cushing, Franklin Steele; Stephen Hanks; and H. H. Sibley papers, Minnesota Historical Society, St. Paul

George B. Merrick papers, State Historical Society of Wisconsin, Madison

Harris family papers and collection, Jo Daviess County Historical Society, Galena

Steamboat collection, Burlington Public Library

Steamboat collection, Putnam Museum and Archives, Davenport

Steamboat collection, Mississippi River Museum, Dubuque

Steamboat collection, Missouri Historical Society, St. Louis

Steamboat collection, Murphy Library, University of Wisconsin–La Crosse

Steamboat collection, St. Louis Mercantile Library, University of Missouri St. Louis

Steamboat collection, Winona Co. Hist. Society

Steamboat ticket collection, Battle of Lexington State Historic Site, Lexington, MO

Way collection, Cincinnati and Hamilton Co. Public Library, Cincinnati

Western Historical Manuscript Collections, State Historical Society of Missouri, St. Louis and Columbia

Index
[Names of boats are printed in italics; boldface indicates a picture.]